What Every Church Member Should Know About Clergy

What Every Church Member Should Know About Clergy

A Practical Guide to Selecting Pastors, Understanding Their Role, and Developing Quality Pastor/Parish Relationships

ROBERT G. KEMPER

The Pilgrim Press
New York

Library of Congress Cataloging in Publication Data

Kemper, Robert G.
What every church member should know about clergy.

Includes bibliographical references.
1. Clergy—Office. 2. Pastoral theology. I. Title.
BV660.2.K475 1985 253'.2 84-22821
ISBN 0-8298-0728-4

The Pilgrim Press, 132 West 31 Street, New York, NY 10001

WITH LOVE TO

the members of the United Church of Christ of
Western Springs, Illinois

They know all of this but still accept me as their pastor.

Contents

PREFACE

How to Use This Book

THIS BOOK is *for* lay people. It is *about* clergy. Its purpose is to provoke, facilitate, and enrich conversations between clergy and lay members about who clergy are and what they do.

Here is a glimpse of the theory that has been used: Healthy churches are churches in which there is a high level of trust between pastor and people. The high level of trust develops through understanding. Some lay member misunderstandings may be false assumptions, indifference, or outright ignorance about clergy. This book intends to clarify and correct the assumptions, dispell indifference, and enlighten church members about ministerial personhood and expectations. Its audience is all who relate to ministers.

The design and layout, as well as the contents, are carefully organized to realize an end purpose: significant conversation between lay people and clergy. This is not a book that a person reads, but one that a person reads and then talks about it. Everything in it prompts and shapes such conversations. Every denominational tradition provides some specific entity for the meeting of the pastor and the parishioners. This entity (and the process of meeting) is called pastor/parish relationships.

The best way to read and discuss this book is from beginning to end because it is structured in such a way as to develop a concept and then to apply that concept in particular circumstances typical of parish life. The lay person may bring a particular interest to it. For instance, what happens to a church when a beloved pastor dies, is disabled, or moves from the congregation? There is a discussion of such untoward circumstances in pastor/parish relationships, but reading about and discussing them will be more satisfying, more productive, if done from the perspective of the concept that precedes the specific circumstance.

No reader agonizes over the words of the text the way the author does. The reader wants to "get something out of" what he or she reads. So, the book is organized to help the reader find what he or she is looking for. First, an extended and descriptive table of contents helps the reader understand where the whole book goes and identifies what he or she wants to know. Second, in the body of the text the reader will find short aphorisms set off in italic type. These are identifying aphorisms, not summaries or introductions. They let the reader know what a particular section is about.

The specific language and general theme of the book do try not to underestimate the reader's intelligence; however, theological and ecclesiastical terminology are kept to a minimum. Clergy may find it disappointing not to begin, for instance, with an exploration of the doctrine of the church. For better or worse, lay people may not start with a priority about such matters. The absence of a preliminary exposition on the doctrine of the church suggests that this is a book about clergy for lay readers.

The most difficult problem for the author is not making theological and ecclesiastical concepts understandable, rather, it is dealing with denominational varieties as they pertain to pastor/parish relationships. The readers, it is assumed, are mainline Protestant parishioners. In faith, liturgy, and sacraments there is an amazing similarity among the churches of mainline Protestantism. But not so with pastor/parish procedures. The resolution of this denominational problem is to focus on the larger process that pertains; the readers must translate how that process works in the churches of their particular denomination. Further, it is assumed that denominational officers are active participants in the discussion of pastor/parish relationships that this book evokes, facilitates, and enriches.

Strangely, perhaps unfortunately, this book does not develop spheres of lay ministries vis-à-vis spheres of ordained ministries. Such careful delineation would be essential to a book on *church* leadership. Without delineating these spheres, or even trying to capture the infinite variety of their intersections, this book assumes that there are both lay and clerical ministries that, together, are the ministries and mission of the church. It aims to interpret the personhood and role of the clergy to lay members. Any attempt at a serious exploration of both forms of ministry would produce another, different book. Maybe someday there will be a companion volume on that complex subject. But for now, the goal is to interpret clergy to lay members in the high hope that such interpretation will provoke significant conversation among these two components of the church.

Finally, this is not an answer book. Opinionated, yes. Wise, maybe. The reader should not be dismayed by my confession that I do not know everything about pastor/parish relationships. One kind of understanding puts Humpty-Dumpty together after the fall; another understanding keeps Humpty's balance stable so that he does not fall. This book pursues stability, not reconstruction. The answers are not "what to do when . . ." answers. The answer this book offers is that pastors and parishioners work together healthily when they understand each other.

Robert G. Kemper
Western Springs, Illinois

Acknowledgments

With appreciation to

Peggy Grosse, who took my messy scribblings and made of them a manuscript;

Margie, who won't let me grumble about things as they are unless I have a better idea of how things might be;

And to the members of our church who trusted me to use a time apart in the wider service of other churches.

R.G.K.

What Every Church Member Should Know About Clergy

INTRODUCTION

An Approach to Pastor/Parish Relationships

THIS BOOK is about the preservation and advancement of healthy churches. It develops a practical theory about healthy churches: The health of a local church is directly related to the quality of the pastor/parish relationship. Mutual understanding and mutual respect between a pastor and a congregation result in healthy churches. Conversely, misunderstanding and disrespect between a pastor and a congregation lead to unhealthy, diseased churches. Health and disease in local churches cross a wide spectrum. Because of the variety of churches and the variety of pastors and because of unique circumstances affecting congregations, no one church is healthy in each and every index of health. As a general proposition, the indices of health are positive when the quality of the pastor/parish relationship is a priority in a congregation.

In any congregation, lay members are the majority, a large majority. Depending on church size, lay members outnumber clergy thirty-five to one—or one thousand to one. It is the nature of a local church to have more lay members than clergy members. The acquisition and exercise of power and authority are *not* numerical. A central theme of this book is that in local churches, power and authority are shared by clergy and laity. Health emerges when clergy and laity have a mutual understanding of the power and authority they share in the church.

The intention of this book is to teach lay members about clergy. Admittedly, there is a measure of haughty pretention in that intention. Lay members know clergy. In the normal course of church participation, lay members know dozens, maybe even hundreds, of clergy. What they know about clergy is what clergy have taught them. Such knowledge may be either positive or negative. It may also be superficial and sketchy. The pastors of the lay people who are learning about clergy may want to say, "That's not me!" Or, "Yes, but . . . " Such rejection or correction is permissible in the framework of this book because of its intended utilization.

The focus is on the "we-ness" of congregational life—the life *together* of lay *and* clergy in a healthy, local church. Unlike other books on Christian life, this book is structured for a *group* of readers. It is designed to provoke discussion between laity and clergy. Therefore, it is highly recommended—even necessary—for a pastor and members of the congregation to read the book and then discuss it together. This is where the rejections and corrections can emerge. It is good to do, for the overall intention is to clarify, through dialogue, the power and authority of clergy and laity in a local congregation.

Another complication in a book that intends to teach lay people about clergy is denominational tradition. Mainline Protestant churches in the United States and in Canada are enough alike that a general description of church life can be employed with near universal understanding. But when the focus requires attention to particularities, there may be some divergence and confusion. For example, titles and proper nouns vary from denomination to denomination. In some churches, clergy are "pastors"; in others, "ministers"; in still others, "priests," "rectors," or just "preachers." And depending on local church polity (system of governance), authorized lay groups relating directly to the clergy may be called "deacons," "pastor/parish committees," "vestry," "session," and so on. The functional roles are sufficiently alike in mainline churches that readers can translate the more familiar vocabulary into their own denominational terms. For the most part, the inclusive term pastor/parish refers to the functional relationships between clergy and lay congregations.

Thus, by whatever names, lay people are provided such material about clergy that they can engage their religious leaders in conversations about who clergy are and what they do, each respectively and both collectively, in Christ's church.

Since this book intends to teach lay people about clergy, it is fitting and proper that I identify myself. I was ordained into the ministry in 1961. I have had three pastorates; the latest has been twelve years in duration. My ministerial specialty is communications, and I have exercised that specialty as an editor, a preacher, and a writer of books. I am a self-appointed advocate of the ministerial profession.

I have about a quarter of a century of experience in the ministry. I am neither a green beginner nor a grizzled veteran. Further, my pastoral experience has been in the latter half of the twentieth century. This means that my mindsets, my vocabulary, my theological and pastoral assumptions are shaped, influenced, and affected by that period's set of cultural landmarks. I have been engaging in religious leadership through a time of assassinations, domestic upheaval, political scandal, rampant inflation, nuclear threats.

I have followed what John Wesley called "the itinerant tradition," meaning a system of one pastor serving sequential, multiple charges or pastorates. This means that I have served in different churches in different communities. My itinerancy has been in small town and suburb, in small, middle-sized, and large churches. Each location, each kind of church has required different leadership skills. The reference to the longer pastorate is also indicative of various ministerial skills required in my career pattern.

No one minister possesses all the skills associated with the ministerial profession. Some clergy are good at one specialty and not so good at others. The discovery and development of particular gifts is part of the dynamic of pastor/parish relationships. Twenty-five years ago I had no idea I would become a writer!

Some clergy resent and resist the term profession; they prefer terms like "calling" and "servant." What they resist and resent are the excesses of professionalism. So do I. However, I persist in calling myself a professional. One reason the assertion of the ministry as a profession is relevant in this introduction is that it takes away some of the mystique that clergy hide behind. The very nature of a profession is that it can be examined critically and self-critically. In their extreme resistance to examination, clergy can maintain that they are accountable only to God. They need not explain to any other human being who they are or what they are doing. God knows they mean well, and to these clergy that is enough. The clergy—and the laity—are accountable to God, but this is a first premise, a criterion for mutual evaluation, not a screen to hide behind. So, the ministry is a profession that can be examined critically and self-critically.

Assuming that the ministry is a profession, I boldly identify myself as an advocate of that profession. This means several things. It means that I am a practitioner of the profession. I am not an abstract theorist; the ministry is my work, my life. And more, to use an ethnic put-down, some of my best friends are clergy. Simply stated: I like ministers. I find them decent, honorable, important human beings doing a difficult task. This credential, I believe, gives me the right to criticize. I want, I expect the best. I am not satisfied with second-rate performances. We all can do even difficult tasks better. So, this book is about the difficult tasks of the ministry. Just because it is sometimes critical of the way those tasks are done does not mean that the task or the performer is inconsequential or incompetent. Rather, it means that this advocate of the profession believes that the good, noble, and holy work of the ministerial profession may be done better.

Finally, let me say that I serve healthy churches. My report is on the process by which quality relationships develop. I will disclose some of my failures and some of the failures of the laity. Health does not mean that we always do everything right. Rather, health means that we have set a priority and that we will pursue it even through some of the difficulties of the tasks we have as a Christian church.

No two clergy are alike. Ministerial variety is the leaven of church life.

Of necessity, I must write in generalities about clergy people and the tasks they perform. Such generalities are deceptive.

The very word clergy conjures up an image. Most likely the image is male, middle-aged, caring, loquacious, interested in religion and—whatever is meant by it—godly. Such images are stereotypical, misrepresenting more than they identify.

Until recently, most ministers have been male; from the Civil War until the 1970s there were only a handful of ordained women in most denominations. Today there is as enormous an influx of women into the ordained ministry as into other vocations. The first result of this influx is some changing vocabulary. The traditional clergyman is becoming a clergy person, either male or female. The traditional minister's wife is becoming a spouse, either a husband or a wife. This development is of considerable import for both the present and the future. I do not want to discuss here the merits of the feminine presence in ministry. It is cited merely as a corrective to the image commonly held of the clergy. In time the image will be without gender.

Clergy are young, middle-aged, and older. They are all these because the ministerial profession is a career. People in the profession are pursuing a career pattern, in most cases (but not all) a lifetime career of forty years. The age of clergy is cited here to debunk a myth. There is no prime time for clergy. What there are, are trade-offs. A young minister may be enthusiastic but short on the wisdom that only experience brings. An older minister may be savvy in the ways of churches but less than enthused about innovations. Lest one thinks that middle-aged ministers are the blending of enthusiasm and wisdom, I hasten to add that most middle-aged ministers are also middle-aged parents and may find their professional interests conflicting with their changing marital and familial patterns. A laity that is engaged in thoughtful dialogue with its pastor recognizes that he or she is in a career pattern with differing needs and strengths at each stage of life.

Some clergy are black. Some are Hispanic. Some are native urbanites and want to remain so. Some clergy are rural natives and either want to remain so or want to change. Some clergy are natty dressers; some have the rumpled look. Some drive imported sports cars; some ride bikes. Some look like dirigibles, filling out their pulpit robes to heavier-than-air proportions; some look as if a sharp blast of air would scatter their scrawny countenances. In short, only a few match the idealized image. This is so obvious as to be hardly worth mentioning, and it would not be mentioned *if* there were no accompanying prejudice against the atypical appearance of clergy. But there is.

Before moving on to more substantive categories of the varieties of clergy, let it be noted that clergy fall victim to the same prejudices with regard to lay people. The prejudices of clergy about lay people may be even more hazardous because clergy—as we will subsequently develop—are group people. Clergy need to conceive a composite of typologies in the conceptualization of their parishes. I simply note here that clergy see parishioners as young/old, male/female, sophisticated/unsophisticated, and so forth through all the typologies of human circumstances. The antidote to both stereotypical prejudices is (a) the meeting in authentic personhood of the types in groups and (b) the celebration of variety as a mutually enriching good.

In more substantive categories of clergy varieties, one can note varieties of skill, interest, and competency. In a slightly different context, the apostle Paul asserted a metaphor for diversity. He spoke in metaphorical terms of a human body. An eye is neither an ear nor a foot. The body needs eyes, ears, and feet. So, too, the church needs differing gifts for leadership. One pastor may be a great preacher, but her urban congregation needs social action to improve the lot of the congregation. One pastor may be a most sympathetic and caring counselor, but he is mush in the pulpit. A minister who is loved and admired by the youth group is often distant and estranged from the older members and vice versa.

Back to the image: Lay people have a composite picture of multiple ministerial skills. Such skills exist only in imaginary abstractions, not in a single individual. The point to make here is that, far from being short of measuring up to the image, lay people do well to use Paul's metaphor. The whole church needs a variety of skills and interests. The prima facie evidence is the disaster of cookie-cutter clergy types. Because churches exist in varieties and there are varieties of lay people, God in divine wisdom has given varieties of clergy. Again, the resolution is neither the abandonment of the image of ministerial skill nor the lamentation of shortcomings; rather, it is the discovery of the strengths of clergy and building on those.

There is a variation on the variety-of-clergy-types theme. It is:

> *No two churches are alike. Versatility is a characteristic of clergy leadership.*

To paraphrase Gertrude Stein, a church is a church is a church. Thus, if you have seen one church, you have seen them all. This is ecclesiastical nonsense. No two churches are identical, not in the same denomination, not in the same town, not in the same neighborhood. Churches, like clergy, exist in a sociological context. Transcending this social context is part of the mission of the church. Its very existence forms categories of church types.

Some churches, for instance, have a long history and tradition. In such churches the preservation of that heritage is highly desirable. Other churches, for comparison, are relatively new and still creating their traditions. Such churches desire innovation and experimentation. Some churches are urban; some have always been so, whereas others have become so through changing sociology. Each church requires a different style of ministerial leadership. Each church has a unique profile, which, in turn, implies a unique profile for the leadership required in that church.

Shifting the focus from the social varieties of the church's context to the ministerial task points toward one of the dynamics of lay/clergy relationship. There is a concept here that is simple to state and difficult to execute. The simple principle is that the task of the church shared by lay and clergy is the Christianizing of the social context.

In plain language, the purpose of the church is to be a Christian presence in the world. But when the social context and the churches in that context are so diverse, how does one evolve a strategy of mission and ministry? This part is complex. The strategizing task is arduous.

My theory is that most lay people will not undertake the task. Instead, they will expect the usual and the familiar. It is a rare church profile, developed when a church is seeking a pastor, that does not cite preaching skill as the most desirable trait for the new pastor. Every church wants an excellent preacher. (Later, when I discuss what goes into the task of preaching, it will be shown why excellent preaching is a rare phenomenon.) It is sufficient to note here that the role of clergy is not just one thing, the same and identical in every circumstance.

Thus one of the difficult tasks of a clergy person is identifying and then offering to a congregation the elements of leadership that are appropriate for that particular congregation. Versatility is the key word for this task. The presentation of versatility is the positive side; conflict over criteria by which clergy performance is measured is the negative side. For example, the laity may criticize a pastor for poor preaching, but since theirs has become a predominantly older congregation and the pastor has chosen to spend time with older people, preaching has suffered.

There is not one type of church; nor is there one type of clergy. The problem with a narrow mind-set about ministerial performance is that if one is insensitive to the varieties, the criterion for evaluation is rigidly narrow. The dialogue between lay and clergy leading to a healthy church must include discussion of what kind of church we are and what kind of leadership is therefore required.

> *Everyone is an expert in evaluating clergy.*
> *Genuine religious leadership is hard to define*
> *because it is derived from the church.*

Evaluating clergy is a popular indoor sport. To a certain extent, the processes of evaluation go on all the time, everywhere. We evaluate the performance of elected officials, doctors, athletes. In that sense, evaluating the pastor of a church is no different.

The big difference is the special nature of religious institutions. One of the rationales for asserting that the ministry is a profession is that ministerial work is done within an institutional context. Just as doctors work within hospitals and lawyers work within courts, so clergy work within churches. However, the informal, casual evaluation of clergy is often individualistic, removed from the context of the church. This kind of evaluation reduces to appearances and demeanor. People like—or do not like—the way they talk, look, or act. The casual expertise in evaluating clergy is often based on personal likes and dislikes.

There is an opposite side of the coin of informal evaluation. This side has to do with the apparent prosperity of the local church. On this subject everyone is an expert. If people come to worship, if the budget is met, if the congregational meetings proceed without rancor, then the minister is doing a good job.

Such institutional evaluation rests on this criterion: The highest good is the preservation of the status quo. Earlier I noted how the social context forms a milieu that produces kinds of churches. Using that same insight it can be said here that those same social forces affect institutional appearances. For instance, a new church in a new retirement community will almost certainly attract members. Yet a traditional Protestant church in a suburban community is rapidly losing members owing to the departure of Protestants and the influx of new residents with a Roman Catholic heritage who are moving into the community from the city. Is the minister in the retirement community more effective, a better leader, than the minister in the suburban community? The answer is yes if the criterion is the preservation of the institutional status quo. But is that a fair and helpful evaluation in these different social contexts?

Management consultant Peter Drucker says that the first question he asks when consulting with an institution is, What are you trying to accomplish? This is a preferable basis for evaluation. It applies to the church as an institution. It also applies to a particular sermon, counseling session, or board meeting. The Drucker criterion reminds the church that it is organized to accomplish a purpose. If no purpose is intended, then there is no need of organization. If the purpose is there, but the church is not reaching it, then the church has a faulty organization.

I have a theory (admittedly unsubstantiated) about harsh criticism of the pastor of a local church. Acknowledging first that some pastors provoke harsh criticism, this does not explain all harsh criticism of pastors. More likely, severe criticism of a particular pastor arises from the frustrations of the critic. The internal soul of the critic is hurting and he or she projects his or her feelings outward, on the pastor. The critic may be experiencing a personal loss through the death of a loved one, the death of a community known and loved for years, the death of a beloved church. The basis of such criticism, then, is internal, not external.

Even in this theory of the origin of harsh criticism the Drucker question is valid. It may be that a troubled church should be attempting to accomplish a decent burial of what has been and to accept the resurrection that is to follow.

The intended point is that clergy evaluation is limited and often unfair if it is personal or institutional. The first step in a quality pastor/parish relationship leading to a healthy church is mutual, realistic goals developed together in a planning process. Realistic goals are the key. It does little good to say that nothing is wrong with this church that one hundred new members wouldn't help.

This may be true, but are there a hundred new members out there and will the congregation assimilate them into their fellowship? Once the pastor and the congregation have mutually agreed on what the organization is trying to accomplish, then both have a stake in its development and each has a way of measuring how the organization is doing in its pursuits. Such goal setting and evaluation of performance within the context of those goals discloses institutional expertise. It certainly is preferable to evaluation based on likes and dislikes or on institutional appearances.

> *The key to quality in pastor/parish relationships is mutual trust.*

What is the general sociological category of a local congregation? It is a voluntary organization. One can argue that the church is different from the country club or the Rotary. In terms of its mission—what it is trying to accomplish—it most certainly is different from other voluntary organizations. Functionally, it is like a voluntary organization.

In American history there is a reason for the church being like a voluntary organization. Most denominations have European origins. Most European progenitors were state churches. The American social experiment did away with a state church. An implication, too little noted, to the separation of church and state principle, as stated in the First Amendment of the Constitution, is what that principle did to organized religion in free societies. One tends to think more about the limitations on government implied in this principle. There are also enormous implications for church organization related to that principle.

American churches are funded by the gifts of their supporters as opposed to governmental taxation. What is more, one chooses to join or not to join a church. In that economic and participatory sense, local churches are like voluntary organizations. (I leave for another discussion the countering argument that church membership is a higher duty and obligation than is club membership.)

If one accepts the assertion that local churches are free and voluntary social organizations, how do such organizations function? The answer is simple but complex: Voluntary organizations function on trust among the participants. The essence of quality pastor/parish relationship is trust. The healthy congregation is the congregation in which the trust levels between the pastor and the congregation are high. This is so easy to see and to say. It is difficult to enact and perpetuate. Because it is so important, let me share some insights into the trust relationship between pastor and congregation. The elements of a trust relationship are:

Mutual accountability. There is a structure of trust. There is a perimeter and a bottom line. For a Christian church, the perimeter and bottom line are Jesus Christ. In this sense the Bible is the rule book for churches. (Yes, there are complications to biblical authority: What does the Bible say? mean? by whom and how interpreted? And how do we enter ecclesiastical tradition into pure biblical authority?) Despite the complications, mainline Protestant churches are accountable to Christ for the maintenance and mission of the church.

Churches use a wonderful shorthand word for this principle of accountability: *covenant.* A covenant is a relationship in which one or more parties pledge to live in a continuing relationship with the other or others. A marriage is a covenant. So is an ordination. So, too, is church membership. When one thinks about it, the church lives by a covenant. Church covenants are historic and contemporary, horizontal and vertical, personal and social.

A pastor/parish relationship is enacted and sustained by

a covenant. The pastor and the congregation share a covenant with Christ. The deepest meaning of Holy Communion is contained in the biblical words used in the liturgy when referring to the cup: "This is the new covenant in my blood." In that sacramental act, laity and clergy renew their covenant with Christ.

A covenant relationship exists between the pastor and the congregation. Sometimes there are written expressions of the covenant, as in some denominational traditions that have a written "terms of call." Rarely does a legal contract exist between a pastor and a congregation. The covenantal relationship means that each, pastor and congregation, pledges to live with the other on the terms of the covenant.

Thus, the covenant relationship is one of mutual trust with common accountability. Yes, sometimes covenants are broken by one or both parties. The Bible is resplendent with stories of covenants broken—and renewed! But on the positive side, covenants are continually operative in relationships as long as the trust level remains. A healthy church is one in which the covenants are made, kept, and remembered.

Spheres of authority. A church covenant expresses a unity of the church but with divisions of authority. The divisions can be complex, but generally, the division of authority confers on the pastor the preaching of the Word and the administration of the sacraments; the laity are charged with the authority of presenting Christ to the world. (Different denominations divide authority in different ways, but this is the usual division.) To be sure, this is a Reformation form from four hundred years ago. Much has changed since then and there are many murky areas of contention between laity and clergy.

The very existence of spheres of authority implies that the tasks of lay and clergy, although both church tasks, are not one and the same task. Indeed, in the history of the church a whole discipline of education has developed to prepare people to exercise the authority of pastors and the authority of lay members.

Often in troubled churches there is the problem of laity encroaching into clergy spheres of authority and of clergy encroaching into lay spheres of authority. The resolution is usually a renegotiated covenant specifying the spheres of authority that exist between the two. The important point here is that there are differing tasks between lay and clergy and they should be acknowledged as being different and as being equally essential to the health of the church.

Communication. Trust relationships survive by communication. Each party must know who the other is, what the other is doing, and what to expect from the other. Most covenants are stretched to the breaking point by failures of communication.

Lay members should know that this form of communication is difficult for clergy. Clergy *know* they are trustworthy; they are reluctant to keep saying so. But saying it is essential. Lay people sometimes forget that lay leadership changes every year. For pastors, this means starting all over again, explaining to new lay leadership who the clergy are and what they do.

No matter what form the communication takes, it is essential. It is essential because its absence is disastrous. Failures of communication about the accountability of the spheres of authority have long-term consequences. If ministers do not tell their congregations who they are and what they do, the congregations may think that their pastors do not know what they are doing or that they are doing the wrong thing.

Constancy. One does not establish a trust relationship

and leave it alone. Such a relationship is fragile and hungry. It will break or starve if not constantly attended. It is the best way to deal creatively with change. Through the years, pastors change and churches change. There should be no surprise in that. The surprise comes when both pastor and congregation realize that they have not communicated over the years and that they have become strangers and distrustful of each other. So, repetitive and boring as it may be, communication must be served in the interest of sustaining trust relationships, which are the essence of quality pastor/parish relationships.

> *Healthy pastor/parish relationships require mutual respect and cooperation.*

Consolidate the random assertions. They are the parts to the puzzle of what constitutes a healthy church. I have been putting together a picture of quality pastor/parish relationships.

The essence of the picture is trust. When one considers the diversity of churches, the diversity of clergy, and the complexities of the tasks, it is a wonder that anything good ever happens in our churches. The opportunities for strife and rancor are great! But just as in medicine the frontier is not in the study of disease, but in the study of health, so, too, in religious organizations the frontier is on healthy relationships based on trust.

Because of the voluntary nature of local churches held together in covenants, the emphasis must be on mutual respect and cooperation. It is my contention that mutual respect and cooperation are by-products of a process. One cannot start by saying clergy and laity must have mutual respect and cooperation. They start by understanding each other.

The first chapter discusses what clergy do. For a pastor, such documentation is familiar territory. It is the stuff of his or her life. But for that pastor and his or her congregation, the recitation of what ministers do is a firm foundation for trust building, leading toward mutual respect and cooperation, which is the sign of a healthy church with pastor/parish relationships of enduring and energizing quality.

CHAPTER 1

What Do Ministers Do?

An Exploration of the Work of Clergy

IF THERE IS ONE JOKE your pastor has heard before—and would be pleased never to hear again—it is the joke about working only twenty minutes on Sunday morning. The clergy's weariness of that joke is not simply that it is untrue or unfunny. The cringe in a minister hearing that reference to his or her work is the cringe of recognizing that the laity do not understand what the minister really does.

The other inaccurate side of the coin is the perception among laity that their minister is a busy person. This expression is heard in the context of asking the minister to do something special for them, or when the minister has made a special effort on their behalf. Usually clergy do not cringe when they hear a reference to their busyness. Clergy assume that the speaker understands, even if vaguely, that they are people with multiple duties and consuming responsibilities.

Curious, is it not, that laity can hold two contradictory perceptions of clergy life and work? Clergy are, on the one hand, indolent in cushy jobs and, on the other hand, frantic busybodies scampering hither and yon, ever doing God's work. The contradictions and the inaccuracies of both propositions tell a truth—some lay people have little reliable perception of what ministers actually do. This is a critical judgment about some laity; they *should* know what ministers do. It is also a critical judgment about clergy. The laity receive their impressions of clergy work from the clergy themselves, and the judgment is that the clergy simply have not taught the laity about the work of the pastor in the local church.

For trust relationships to develop, such misunderstandings must be corrected. Faulty assumptions about what clergy actually do—or should do—result in faulty evaluations and unrealistic expectations. This is obvious in the case of lay perceptions of clergy. It is not so obvious, but nonetheless effective, in the case of clergy perceiving themselves in relation to the laity. In both directions, then, the miscalculation of clergy work has harmful consequences in trust relationships. In this chapter I want to provide descriptions that will lead to substantive dialogue between lay and clergy about the work clergy do.

There are some problems in defining the work of clergy. I define the work of clergy in two categories: presence and performance. The second category is readily understandable and easy to observe and evaluate. Most parish ministers perform six functions in a parish church. These functions will be delineated with precision and clarity. But the first category, that of presence, is harder to define and delineate. Yet it must be cited in an exploration of what clergy do. They are a pastoral presence in the church and in the world. It can be asserted that presence precedes performance. That is, the "who-ness" of the ministerial person is the foundation on which the structure, with particular functions, arises. The ministerial presence is intangible, elusive to precise definitions, even mystical. Its manifestations are in the realms of symbols and images. It is debatable, in the technical sense, whether or not this ministerial presence is work. I say it is, on the grounds that it is unique to the tasks of religious leadership and that the ministerial presence is prelude to ministerial performance. In short, being a presence is an important part of what clergy do.

> *Ministerial work is first and foremost representational work.*
> *The minister is a symbol to the congregation of who they are.*

If clergy want to find some redeeming, positive element in the cracks about twenty minutes on Sunday morning, they can take some small comfort in the insight that the preaching moment on Sunday morning is the tip of the larger, submerged entity concerning their tasks. The minister in the pulpit on Sunday morning is visible, identifiable as person and professional, and the model of some aspects of Christianity to the congregation.

Clergy will shy away from those words. They sound like a Christian on a pedestal, and they want no part of pseudoidolatry. On the surface, such talk sounds presumptuous and pretentious. Maybe it is to clergy. It may very well be prideful and arrogant for the clergy to think of themselves in this way; however, this is not an insight about how clergy see themselves, but of how the laity perceive clergy work.

Clergy work is *representational.* Break the word down into its component parts—*re-pre-sent.* Seen this way, it is a good biblical concept. It is about mission, being sent. It is about being before people. It is about repetition and recreation. This modeling role is strictly professional; it has nothing to do with the merit or virtue of the person. Clergy who can handle this representational role generally are clergy who use it not to attract attention to themselves, but to attract attention to the reality of God in all of life.

If clergy are disturbed by the importance I place on this

representational work, let them think of it in another context. When a clergy person enters a hospital or nursing home room, she or he enters it not just as caring neighbor and friend, although she or he may well be that. Rather, the clergy person enters that room with the representational role wrapped all around her or him. It is seen and understood by the patient. How often do the patients want to tell about their absence from church and their high resolve to do better as soon as they are able? Why do they want to tell that to the clergy person? It is because her or his representational role is showing. They see the clergy person as a representative of the church and what the church stands for. The visitation of the sick is cited only as an example of the power of representational work done by clergy. How that image is handled in the sickroom is a matter of pastoral skill. At this point you are invited only to accept the premise that a facet of clergy work is representational.

Thanks to the influence of advertising in our culture we tend to think of images and symbols as somehow crass and evil tools for manipulation. They certainly can be, even in churches. Contemporary psychology, especially the insights of Carl Jung, has explored the internal perceptive process in human beings who use what Jung called "universal mythical typologies." We understand in terms of images and symbols, representing complex, diversified, maybe even frightening realities. In short, this is serious, substantive work.

So far, this assertion has been cautious about the content of the image or role model that clergy convey. Yes, they represent the congregation. But the congregation is a repository of historic beliefs. This is mixed and complex, but clergy have in their representational work thoughts, perceptions, and experiences held by people about all that is religious—God, Jesus, the Bible, the sacraments. There was once a shorthand definition of clergy as "A Man of

God." In today's language such a term is too unmystical, meaning that we have so many definitions of God that the phrase blurs rather than focuses meaning. But in terms of representational work, that is profound: The primary work of the clergy is to represent religion in all its dimensions to people.

> *Representative people are still people. Their images are created images, but their images are also inherited.*

Lay people should know that the representative work of clergy is twenty-four-hour-a-day work. Think about it. When a lay person meets her or his minister away from the church and wants to introduce the minister to a friend, does she or he not always cite name *and* title? The lay person will say, "Meet Reverend Smith, my minister." Will she or he also say, "Meet Herb Jones, my plumber"? Not likely. Why not? Because she or he sees the person and the role simultaneously.

In the social sciences there are two forms of status: acquired and inherited. The Queen of England has inherited status. She is treated with respect because she is the queen. An athlete has acquired status, earned from fans by being good at what he or she does. The status of clergy is both acquired and inherited. A new pastor in town is the recipient of inherited status. It is conferred on him or her by virtue of his or her position in the church. It is the sum of what that church expects its minister to be. Tentative and conditional trust is given to the newcomer, but the newcomer must also prove to be worthy of that trust. This is where the acquired status comes from. Does this representative person deserve the trust of the office? Time will show whether acquired status can be added to inherited status.

This, too, is work. The church's shorthand phrase for

this is "getting to know the people." It describes the process of acquiring status. The process means meeting the people in multiple circumstances. It means presenting yourself to the people in a way that invites their trust and confidence. Some of this is done publicly, as in the leadership of worship. Some of it is done informally, as in affable chitchat with people.

The power of this representational work is disclosed in its dysfunction. If a minister does something ingratiating or irritating to a congregation or a person, the minister will see how a trust image can shatter and scatter. A new Caucasian minister in a Hawaiian congregation made a casual remark on noticing that a Japanese parishioner had come to a party without his wife. The Japanese thought that such a remark impugned his marriage and threatened a defamation of character lawsuit!

But there is also a positive side to representational work. To isolate just one positive component, clergy who present themselves as being knowledgeable about a particular subject, sacred or secular, usually are deferred to in an area of competence. A minister in a congregation who had previously been a certified public accountant received unaccustomed deference from the church treasurer in matters of finance.

The point of this exploration of clergy work as representational is a reminder to lay and clergy about the complexity of the dynamic between the personal and the professional. Paul's phrase about "treasures in earthen vessels" is a helpful one to have in mind. Clergy are people. Their humanity must be acknowledged. It is a disservice to them and to the church to think of clergy in pedestal terms. Their work, however, requires certain aspects of character. Foremost among these is trustworthiness. The corrective to thinking too highly or too lowly of clergy is simply knowing that one's perception of clergy is both mythical and realistic. Healthy pastor/parish relationships are those in which the presence of the mythical and real are acknowledged and an effort is made to find congruities in the two.

Being a presence to a congregation in this sense of representational work is sometimes a burden to clergy. To be sure, representational work is not a high priority of the day-to-day routines that clergy follow, but it is always there. It becomes a burden to clergy in that it forms a criterion of self-evaluation. Clergy judge themselves on how well they have represented God, Christ, the Bible, the sacraments to the congregation. By this standard of self-evaluation they almost always find themselves deficient and short of the mark. Their burden is a gnawing sense of failure no matter the apparent signs of well-crafted work in the institutional church. Because the standards are high, there is always room for failure! Earthen vessels are inadequate containers of all that is holy. Paul knew that. So should laity and clergy.

> *The style of leadership required for pastors of local churches is often at odds with other norms of leadership.*

I have explored the first component of the ministerial presence in pastoral terms. The second component is in institutional terms. The ministerial presence, what clergy do, in this second category is the leadership of a religious institution.

The form of leadership in a local church has denominational variations. By constitutional mandate and historical tradition, some clergy are presiding officers of local churches. Other clergy, following other historical patterns, are ex officio leaders, outside the constitutional decision-making process of the local church. Either way, this is an area in which the spheres of authority between laity and clergy intermingle and, in whatever historical form, are shared. Both lay and clergy participate in the decision-making process, or power structure, of a local church. Needless to say, this is often an area of conflict between lay and clergy. Despite high potential for conflict and despite denominational variations, both lay and clergy understand that what ministers do is *lead* a congregation. But after agreeing that clergy are religious leaders, questions of how to lead a congregation and how to share leadership are often areas of disagreement.

Leadership itself, in whatever context—business, governmental, educational—is hard to define and execute. In a sense, the only true judge of leadership is history. At some future point one can look back and say, "There, in that moment, leadership was present." This is little help to clergy in that moment. No one can anticipate fully the consequences of decisions made in a given moment.

Leadership is conceived of as an "in-front" position; that is, the leader is at the apex of the pyramid, the director of the subordinate legions, the one who is responsible for the whole enterprise. Therefore, in general terms, such leadership appears as sound direction, confident assurance of directions undertaken, decisions made on behalf of the common good of the organization. Sometimes clergy picture their leadership role in these terms. Sometimes, too, laity evaluate pastoral leadership in these terms. Generally, when such leadership conforms to the expectations and desires of the laity, it is looked on approvingly. But when such leadership does not conform to the laity's expectations and desires, conflict develops. Common symptoms of such leadership conflicts are the division into "we" and "they" groups, complaints about "railroading" decisions, and ad hominem attacks on the leader. A sure sign of conflict between lay and clergy over church leadership is when the conversation focuses on personalities and style of leadership rather than on the merits of the issues requiring decision.

Consider an alternative conceptualization of pastoral leadership. Other norms of leadership are of dubious value because they require a hierarchical structure for enactment. The shape of a church is more spherical than pyramidal. An implication of that geometric conception is that leadership cannot be by directive, from the top down. Rather, leadership must permeate the whole sphere, and consensus must emerge among the constituency. There is a secular, vocational model for this form of leadership. The model is that of a politician.

If this sounds too "smoke-filled roomish," consider: A politician has power and authority from the consent of the governed. The political leader must serve the electorate, the constituency. So, too, a pastor of a local church must serve the congregation. But does the leader only serve that constituency? Can he or she not also move that constituency to new territory? Yes, the leader can but not by directive. There are, in political leadership, "hacks" and "statesmen." A hack just plays on the needs, fears, and prejudices of the constituency. A statesman stays in touch with the constituency but moves them onward. The movement may be by example, by persuasion, by rhetoric. In whatever manner, the statesman builds a clamor in the constituency for what they ought to do. Is this hard to do? It most certainly is. Is this possible to do? Yes, but it is difficult and takes longer. It is my assertion that effective pastoral leadership is political-like, serving a constituency while moving them into new territory.

The political model may be applicable to all forms of voluntary organizations, but here the focus is on the church. Churches have "given" goals and objectives. They come from the Christian tradition, expressed in scripture and church history. However it is expressed, churches are the extensions of the mission of Jesus Christ. Ministry, both lay and clergy, is also an extension of the ministry of Jesus Christ. The criterion for church leadership is the criterion of faithfulness to the ministry of Jesus Christ.

A troublesome element of that heritage is the word servant. It is an honored biblical noun. The self-conception of clergy is closely tied to that word. They think of themselves, as their stoles symbolize, as servants of Christ. In contemporary parlance, the servant is of low estate, the bottom of the social pyramid. Functionally, this often means that whatever anyone tells the servant to do, the servant does—and does it gladly and obediently. In the life of the contemporary church this is a confusing status. Really, it is more like the expectations one has for a well-trained house pet.

Ernest T. Campbell, professor of homiletics at Garrett Evangelical Theological Seminary in Evanston, Illinois, offers a corrective sentence: "They also serve who lead." The attraction of this sentence is that it expresses the proper humility of religious leadership. The whole church, lay and clergy, is subordinate to Christ. The whole church is composed of Christ's servants in the world. This servanthood forms a context for lay and clergy leadership. Both lay and clergy have derived power and authority, derived from servanthood to Christ. I therefore disapprove of haughty, mountaintop leadership for local churches. I approve of dreams and visions of the Christian traditions that are taken so seriously that they are infused within the life of a whole congregation until the people move toward those dreams and visions. That is how clergy lead. That is the ministerial presence in a church. That is what clergy do.

Before moving beyond these representational works it should be noted that in healthy churches, leadership is not singular, the isolated work of the pastor. Functionally, in the day-to-day life of a local church, leadership is shared, collectively, with the laity. Some are helped by the phrases "leader of leaders" and "enabler of the congregation." Unhealthy churches are those in which decision-making and direction-setting are the sole prerogatives of the clergy. Often clergy leadership is a mediating role, negotiating and interconnecting other centers of leadership. But that is an insight about the particular form of ministerial leadership, not necessarily contradictory to the representational task of ministerial leadership.

The second category of what clergy do is performance. Be not deceived by the word performance. It may connote a more theatrical sense than is intended. The intended meaning of the word here is in the sense of discharging tasks, just as high-performance automobiles are those that do with ease the tasks they are expected to perform. Just as clergy work done as presence is an exploration of the "who-ness" of ministers, so clergy work as performance is an exploration of the specific "what-ness" ministers do.

Some years ago Samuel Blizzard of Harvard Divinity School published an article in *The Christian Century* that was an inquiry into ministerial work. Over the years Blizzard's categories have become a standard for the functional categories of what ministers do. The following is a commentary on the six functional areas in which ministers perform in the local church.

1. *Preaching.* Pastors of local churches preach to their congregations. The centrality of preaching is part of the Protestant heritage. As noted earlier, in remarks defining the spheres of ministerial authority, most mainline denominations employ "the preaching of the Word" as a definition of ministerial authority. Here I would note that preaching is one of the tasks that ministers perform.

Fairly or unfairly, pastors are evaluated on their preaching skills. When seeking a new pastor, most congregations cite preaching ability as their highest priority. It is a bit deceptive for congregations to do this. The deception is congregational self-deception. Congregations tend to think that quality preaching is something done out of the minister's hip pocket and that he or she can do it while performing with distinction all the other tasks expected of ministers. It is also self-deceptive unless the congregation fully intends to support by attendance, feedback, and understanding what preachers do.

> *Quality preaching is such an all-consuming discipline that those pastors who are quality preachers are usually just that and no more.*

In fairness to congregations there is a solid reason for the high priority they place on preaching skills. The task of preaching is highly visible work and it is self-revelatory. When congregations say that they want their pastor to be a good preacher they may mean that they want to see in their pastor an approachable person, a warm and understanding person, a person they can trust. Congregations have an uncanny ability to discern the character of a pastor through his or her preaching. By listening and watching, laity can tell what preachers care about and how they relate religion to life and can determine their views of scripture and the approach they take to accomplishing tasks. This is a lot to discern. Admittedly, there is a large margin for error in this evaluative process, but that is part of what lay people receive from their preacher's words and demeanor.

Another reason congregations place a high priority on preaching: It is a congregational event. All the members, and often the larger community too, encounter the preacher in the pulpit. Other ministerial tasks apply most directly to segments of the congregation, but preaching is to the whole congregation. So, when congregations say they value good preaching, they are transcending their personal interests and saying that "we all, the brothers and sisters of this congregation," need to hear the Word of God with power and authority.

The preceding two points help to clarify what the lay member expects from the preacher of his or her congregation. But before moving on to other ministerial tasks, let me sharpen the understanding of the preaching task.

Preaching is a communications art. The modes of communication change. Preaching emerged in a preliterate society. Today communication is not only literate, but also visual. The contemporary mind is set to receive thousands of stimuli. One voice droning on may not be sufficiently stimulating to the contemporary mind.

Quality preaching arises from discerning listening.

Further, there is a "how to" component and a "what to" component in the art of communications. Quality preaching is the happy marriage of the two. But it is possible for a pastor to have only one of those components. On the one hand, some preachers know how to be very entertaining, very dramatic, very sincere. Those are techniques of communication, not preaching itself. On close analysis, such preachers may be empty. As Shakespeare might have put it, their words are "full of sound and fury signifying nothing." On the other hand, some preachers lack the techniques of communication but have something important to say. They do not know how to pace a sermon, how to illustrate a sermon, or how to structure a sermon for audience reception. They may even lack certain basic skills of speech formation and projection.

Before judging a pastor's preaching too harshly, lay people should know that their impatience with preaching may be a cultural phenomenon—how many of us can listen to a twenty-minute speech without our attention wandering? Perhaps a preacher has mastered only part of the communicator's art. The laity should know that preaching skill is not a prerequisite for ordination. There is no sample sermon that is judged by some board, leading to certification. Moreover, the priority for skill in preaching is not nearly as high in theological seminaries as it is in local churches. Some clergy may graduate from accredited seminaries but have little practical experience in preaching (homiletics, as it is called in seminary). The laity should know that the seminaries are right when they say that preaching cannot be taught. (What the seminaries mean, of course, is that effective preaching begins as a gift of God to a person, and in the stewardship of a person the gift is developed in a lifetime of practice.) The point to the laity is that preaching is a task in the process of development. No pastor, no matter how mature, has learned all there is to know about preaching. The pastor to worry about is the pastor who has stopped trying to learn to improve, to experiment.

The art of preaching has been in a time of eclipse. There are, however, signs of its reemergence. Lay people have an important role to play in that reemergence. Frankly, it is not enough for lay people to say, "Our minister cannot preach." What is required is some honest feedback to the pastor about his or her preaching. Such feedback must be constructive, offering particular suggestions about the better use of theme and technique. Lay feedback is encouraged because preaching is a corporate, not an individual, act. It requires active listening.

The discernment of lay people can be broadened, too, by their recognition that there are different, legitimately different, kinds of sermons. They may all sound alike, but sermons are in fact very different. Some sermons take a text from the Bible and expand that text. Some sermons are topical, bringing the resources of the Christian tradition to bear on a particular topic. Some sermons inform; some persuade; some comfort; some challenge. Like

Drucker's question to organizations, lay people do well to evaluate a sermon by asking, "What was it trying to accomplish?"

Preaching is not just like all other forms of public speaking.

Finally, consider an *insider's view* about preaching. Every person has in him or her at least one good speech. Theoretically, if that one speech were good enough, it could be given over and over to different audiences. That is what orators on the Chautauqua circuit used to do. But preaching is directed to *the same* congregation week after week. The audience does not change, so the sermon must. This means a new and fresh address every week. They cannot all be winners. A preacher does well to have three or four really good sermons a year.

There is no other way to put it: Preaching in the pastoral context is just plain hard work. It is consuming work. It takes every ounce of energy and imagination the preacher can muster. It means an ever-deepening knowledge of scripture and theology (this means study time), an ever-deepening awareness of the presence of God (this means devotional time), an ever-increasing awareness of the hurts and hopes of the congregation (this means pastoral time). Preaching effectively takes a lot of time. The general rule is one hour of preparation for every minute preached (a twenty minute sermon—twenty hours of preparation).

And never forget that preaching is always in the context of worship. Here's a tip: If it is self-disclosure of the pastor the lay person seeks, he or she should listen more to the pastoral prayer than to the sermon. The lay person should also look to the selection of worship materials. Is there an integrated wholeness to the music, the scripture, the litanies, the printed prayers? Or are they just casually selected and included at random?

Certainly, preaching is an important functional task of the clergy in a local church, but there is more to preaching than meets the ear.

2. *Priest.* Some people may be jarred by the word priest in reference to mainline Protestant clergy. Roman Catholic clergy are called priests. So are some Episcopalian clergy. Orthodox churches have priests. But whoever heard of a Protestant priest? Blizzard insisted upon the word as being descriptive of an important task Protestant clergy perform. If the noun priest throws a roadblock in the way of understanding, try using it as an adjective, as in priestly functions. Protestant clergy do perform priestly functions.

Every local church has rites and rituals to mark the stages or passages of human life. At birth (or in some denominations at young adulthood) there is baptism. At early adulthood there is confirmation. The union of two persons into a family is marriage. Death is ritualized in a funeral or a memorial service. Throughout life, Christians gather around the table for the Lord's Supper, Holy Communion, or the eucharist. These church rituals are benchmarks in the maturation of people and they signify a new status for the person. Some churches call all these rites sacraments; other churches call only baptism and communion sacraments and others "services" or "ordinances." Also, theologically, these events are expressions of the grace of God. The focus in this section of clergy work, however, is not on theological or denominational meaning. Rather, it is on the person who performs these priestly acts on behalf of the congregation.

Earlier, clergy work was described as representational work. In the rites and rituals of the church the clergy do represent the church and its traditions of faith. In the churches of the Reformation these rituals are responses to the grace of God. They are neither miraculous nor mystical, except in the sense that the grace of God is miraculous and mystical. Further, in the churches of the Reformation the value and validity of these rituals do not depend on the righteousness of the clergy, but on the faith of the believers.

> *A parish priest tends to see all life as response to the grace of God.*

Most churches just expect their ministers to perform these tasks. Most clergy feel very ministerial in performing these tasks. Often the ritual is expressed in the words of a service book, and the pastor, inserting the proper names in the ritual, does it "from the book." It would appear that priestly work, then, is easy and simple. But as with everything professional, it is easy and simple when the officiant knows what he or she is doing. Therefore, take a "behind-the-altar" look at what priestly work entails.

First, before one ever picks up a service book to read the ritualistic words, a mastery of tradition and theology is required. Why does the church do these acts? What did Jesus mean when he instituted the special meaning of the Passover meal? What was the symbolism of water (baptism) in an arid country? If Jesus did not perform a funeral service, why does the church? These questions are matters of intellectual and spiritual inquiry. The parish priest should have some clear understanding of the whys and wherefores of these rituals.

Second, there are techniques to these rituals. Where does one stand and how does one use the position of hands in these rituals? Should there be a wedding rehearsal, and who does what at the rehearsal? Such questions may appear trivial. In the greater scheme of things they are, but in the ignorance of church meanings and techniques, great harm can be done by the unprepared.

Third, and most important, the parish priest prepares

people for these rituals. Perhaps the most obvious example of preparation is time spent with a confirmation class. Often a pastor will spend a year or two preparing confirmands for their confirmation. Rarely is a wedding, a funeral, or a baptism done without consultation with those who are involved. For some clergy, such occasions are opportune teaching moments. They want to have a personal relationship with the participants.

The point is that what may seem to the uninformed, casual observer a simple, ten-minute service may represent years of study and hours of preparatory work with the participants. Repeat that over and over and one has a large block of ministerial time. Some clergy contend that a simple wedding ceremony represents about twenty hours of work when premarital counseling, rehearsals, dinners, and receptions are included.

Finally, one is deceived if one thinks that all priestly work is public. Most priestly work is private. The recitation of rituals did not include anointment, unction, and confession. Most Protestant churches have eliminated those as rituals, but their presence continues in priestly work. Clergy "hear confession" all the time, but it is not called that. The visitation of the sick may not include the anointment of the body with oil, but the care for the sick is most assuredly a priestly function.

The biblical image of priestly work is a shepherd. In an urban society one wonders if this is a meaningful image. But priestly work is the care of a group of people, meeting them in the changes of time and ever pointing them toward the grace of God that saves and renews their lives through time and beyond.

3. *Counselor.* Since the 1920s, pastoral counseling has grown steadily in importance. Indeed today, for some clergy, it is the very essence of ministry. It is what they do best, what they most want to do, what they rank as their

highest professional priority. Pastoral counseling has risen in importance in this period because it coincides with the development of knowledge in the whole field of behavioral sciences. An interesting theory about the wide diffusion of pastoral counseling in the United States is that the centers of behavioral sciences were urban centers, often universities, but churches with clergy were in almost every small hamlet of the land. In this century, ministers have become quasi-missionaries, bringing the latest psychological theory to the outposts of the land. Be that as it may, this century has seen a rapid acceleration in ministerial work in the area of counseling. It is a veritable subprofession within the larger context of clergy.

Most lay people expect their pastors to be resources for problems they cannot handle themselves. Problems of child raising and marriage, as well as work-related problems, find their way into the offices of clergy. Ministers are assumed to be understanding and supportive of people struggling with the vicissitudes of life. Historically, ministers were counselors of spiritual problems, but with the advent of psychology in the seminary curriculum, an increasing number of clergy have attempted a wide range of mental health consultations. In one sense, this is beneficial to parishioners. Personal problems are often better confronted in the context of a caring group of peers. It is not unusual for churches to have support groups of people who are struggling to cope with common problems from divorce to death. On a more positive note, churches have a special opportunity to do preventive mental health. Certainly, under the practiced eye of an experienced pastoral counselor, people with emotional instabilities can be identified and, in some instances, helped in the early stages of mental ill health.

People with personal problems have all the time in the world.

Most pastoral counselors are best at diagnosis. They can differentiate between temporary stress and a severe psychosis requiring hospitalization. This is a helpful screening process. Also, clergy, in their roles as preachers and institutional leaders, may become more relevant in relating to people's needs through their role as counselors. Seeing the hurt and hunger in people often prompts sermons and programs aimed at healing the hurt and feeding the deeper hungers.

The lay person, however, should know some consequences of pastoral counseling. In the first place, it takes a lot of time to help a person through a difficult situation. Rarely does one quick conversation make a difference. Helping people back to the status quo in their lives takes many, many hours. In the main, churches want their pastors to do just that. They may underestimate how long this takes, but by and large, they think such work should be undertaken by their pastors.

There is another, more serious consequence to extensive pastoral counseling by pastors of local churches. Serious counseling is de-energizing. It takes a lot out of the minister. It is not just time; it is also sheer strength, enthusiasm, buoyancy. It is the price of caring. Certainly, pastors are most helpful to people by staying objective and not attempting to solve problems that people must resolve for themselves. Still, an afternoon of personal woes, even if heard objectively, is a draining day. "Bearing one another's burdens" can affect the pastor's own mental health.

4. *Teacher.* The parish pastor is usually the master teacher of the congregation. All churches have educational programs, usually for all ages. The most visible and familiar is the Sunday school, customarily staffed by lay volunteers. The clergy are considered a resource to the lay staff.

Often the pastor teaches the confirmation class. Bible study and adult education are usually under the tutelage of the pastor. Often the pastor of a local church is like a public school principal, sizing up curriculum, procuring necessary aids, inspiring teachers, and generally creating a climate for learning in the church.

In truth, the church, the whole congregation, are teachers. One can instruct and instruct in the virtue of loving one's neighbors, but only when a neighbor is rejected or accepted by a congregation does the instruction come to life. So, the pastor's role as a teacher far exceeds just classroom events. Christian education is an enterprise of the whole church and the pastor is its primary merchandiser.

The computer age has given us the slogan "Garbage in, garbage out." Anyone who has spent a moment in an instructional situation should understand that slogan, for it applies also to teaching and learning. One's own knowledge can go so far; it must be replenished. So, in this section on the teaching task, one must also note the learning tasks of pastor-teachers. It may have been ever thus, but it seems as if today's knowledge explosion makes one run rapidly just to stay abreast of current thinking in all areas of religious and secular inquiry.

A virtually unanimous guilt is shared by clergy about their own scholarship. They will confess and complain about not having time to read and learn for themselves. There is reality to this guilt. It is not easily resolved. The congregation does not clamor for disciplined scholarship in its clergy. When it comes to learning, the congregation does not press for or demand this of their pastors. It is more sinister than that. The truth is churches expect it without specifying that it be done. The subtlety is that the absence of scholarly pursuits never appears right away; it has a residual effect. "The pastor's preaching is stale," members will say. "We are doing the same old thing in Sunday school," they will say. Why not? Little new in, little new out.

> *Christian education is like secular education, but the intended end is not the love of learning: It is the love of life.*

Like preaching, teaching has been eclipsed in local churches. But like preaching, it shows signs of renewal. Local churches are uniquely positioned for a particular educational approach. Unlike public education, church education is not restrained from teaching values, morals, and ethics and teaching from a conspicuously religious stance. Further, in an age of specialized and narrow inquiry, Christian education is positioned to be an integrative education. Christian education asks this consolidating question: What does all that mean for the good life?

5. *Organizer.* Blizzard called this aspect of ministerial work organizer, but today we would borrow a business word and call this task, planning. By whatever name, this is a necessary task for institutional life.

Let me illustrate the nature of this task with a personal recollection. When I was a magazine editor, friends seeking to make conversation would ask, "How is the magazine doing?" I always stumbled when the question was asked because of what was in my mind. What was in my mind was the edition of the magazine that was in the mail to the subscriber, the next edition that had just been put on the press, the next edition that we were editing in the office, the next edition in which we were deciding what to include, the next edition that was being solicited, and the next edition or series of editions we were dreaming about doing.

In exploring the necessity of planning in churches, the magazine illustration is pertinent. Institutions exist in the same processes of time as do individuals. An institution has a past, a present, and a future. The work of the clergy in planning has relevance to all three aspects of time. The problem for clergy is that past and present considerations dominate. It is difficult to anticipate tomorrow when one is fully occupied with today. Simply stated, the planning task of clergy requires a split-level mind—one level on the present and another on the future.

> *Religious institutions are inherently conservative and will repeat themselves until pressed to change.*

Laity and clergy are often in conflict over the planning process in a church, and for good reason. Lay members tend to find their meanings of the church in the past. They remember where they went to Sunday school, where they were married, and how they worshiped. Clergy, pursuing a career in religious leadership, tend to value the future more than the past. They dream of how the church might be someday. Planning may begin with a dream, but its fruits are born when steps are taken to marshal the resources needed for the realization of the dream.

For better or worse, clergy are the primary planning officers of a local church. One reason they must function in this way is to protect the church from special interests. Every church has (at least) a group that promotes music, or education, or missions, or the preservation of the building. In the process of decision-making in churches, those groups vie for the available resources. Clergy with oversight of the whole church need a comprehensive strategy for integrating those special interests into the life of the whole church. This comprehensive strategy is planning.

6. *Administration (management).* Blizzard called the sixth functional category of ministerial work administration. Today it might be called management. By whatever name, the task of guiding, coordinating, refereeing, consolidating the resources of a local church toward some comprehensive intended end must be done.

Regardless of the size of the church, there are certain specific elements of management that devolve upon the church's pastor. The first of these elements is personnel management. This may be a paid staff (secretary, custodian, etc.), but more likely personnel management consists of recruiting, training, supervising, and appreciating volunteers. In most churches a nominating committee operates to procure lay officers for the institution. Clergy are often advisers to the nominating committee. Once selected, these lay officers look to the clergy for on-the-job training. Inevitably, when they are confronted with a problem they cannot handle, they want to talk it over with their pastor.

Buildings and grounds become a second element of ministerial management. Universally, this is a lay responsibility, but the minister is in the building daily and is the immediate observer of the building, the contact person when work is to be done, and, if he or she lives in a parsonage or manse, the mediator between the family and the board of trustees.

A third element of management is financial. Every institution has to have a plan for spending and receiving money to meet its objectives. Universally, a treasurer and lay officers are responsible for the financial process. Most clergy understand that in churches the pattern of the flow of the money is the pattern of church power. (Among clergy there is a helpful piece of peer advice: Never miss the budget meeting when a handful of trustees decide the destiny of the church for a year!)

Lay people should know that clergy have great ambivalence about church management. In most church polities they are outside the established structure for lay direction of the church (thus, they have no decisive power). But if something goes wrong, the clergy will be held accountable (thus, they have the responsibility of management). This dilemma of church management is awkward, but in the long run it is probably the best way. The church is a lay organization and the laity should be responsible for its management. In their oversight status the clergy are helpful in communicating the concerns of one part of the church to another and in envisioning the implications for the church.

Management is the art of doing the important.

The need for church management is ample evidence of the urbanization of the church. If you ever explore old church buildings, you will rarely find a church office in the building. In the rural society of a previous day, clergy did not have to be church managers. The older model of the church was that of a fellowship of kindred souls. They met in the church for worship and to mark rites of passage. Today almost every church provides an office or study for its pastor. Such provision symbolizes the contemporary nature of the church and its clergy. Indeed, a study on the church and its ministry coined a term that is descriptive of clergy work.* The study called the clergy "pastoral directors." Put the emphasis on pastoral and one has an insight into the work of the clergy in the administration of a local church.

In his research about the practice of ministry in these six functional categories, Blizzard found that clergy spent the most time in and had the least satisfaction from doing

*H. Richard Niebuhr et al., *The Purpose of the Church and Its Ministry* (New York: Harper & Row, 1956).

administration. (Blizzard's research is outdated, but one suspects this finding would still be true.) Even calling administration "management" has not blurred its repetitive nature. Twenty-five years of monthly trustees' meetings will dull anyone's senses!

An underappreciated factor in church management is the annual replacement of church lay officers. For the pastor, this means starting over every time with a new board and new officers. The older the pastor or the longer the tenure in a particular pastorate, the greater the boredom with the repetitive nature of the tasks. Presumably, this is also true of almost every line of work. But the inherent conservatism of local churches and the necessity of repetition often dull the cutting edge of imaginative and innovative church management. For some clergy, dulled by this phenomenon, management becomes a time-consuming bore.

The six Blizzard categories of ministerial work omitted one important category. (The category was omitted because the study was about the work of ministers *within* local churches.) The additional category of ministerial function is that of *extraparochial ministry.* In addition to their parish responsibilities, most ministers are involved beyond the local parish. Such involvements may include denominational activities, institutional boards, or community services.

Clergy are community resources too.

Some of the nonparochial involvements may be controversial. Some clergy, for instance, have found their way into partisan politics; or into sensitive areas in the community, like an embattled school board; or into social action projects not endorsed by the entire congregation. Such involvements point up an important dimension of clergy work. Clergy are not people to be kept on the parochial reservation. They are, in the largest sense, community resources. Their residence in a community, their special talents or special interests are a community resource. It is difficult—and one could add undesirable—for lay people to divide clergy work into parish work and extraparochial work. Often lay people object if the "outside" work seems to be to the neglect of "inside" things. But a wiser view is that of the interconnectedness of all things. A local church is part of a denomination, a community, a nation. Efforts on behalf of the larger entities usually have effects in all the interconnections of modern life.

The really challenging part of the ministry is doing all these tasks simultaneously.

There are two major learnings to retain in summarizing the presence and the performance of the clergy. The first learning is the recognition of the enormous scope of clergy work. Pastoral work is not just one thing; it is many diverse works. The diversity of the work requires equally diverse talents and skills. Each task is relatively simple and clear; the truly challenging part of clergy work is pursuing all these tasks simultaneously. A typical ministerial day will include aspects of each of the seven functional tasks and the representational works. Often there is little separation between these. They are held together by the pastor's personal integrity.

When lay people evaluate clergy performance, they do well to have in mind the variety of works that pastors perform. It is virtually impossible that there would be uniformity of pastoral skill and competency in all seven functional areas. Lay people might better evaluate clergy by separate categories. If the preaching seems thin or shallow, there may be great depth in counseling or managing.

The final learning is that the seven function areas are

historically the *church's* ministry. The historic, institutional little church on the corner preaches and teaches, cares for souls, preserves and perpetuates its life that it may affect the larger communities of human society. Clergy are not the active agents in this ministry; the church is. The single and primary work of the clergy is to see that these ministries take place. Too often clergy assume that they must do them all. This assumption leads to a deadly clericalism in the churches. God gives gifts for ministry to all human beings. The church invites all to contribute their gifts. The clergy have the gift and hence the responsibility of pastoral oversight.

Thus, it is not through the concentration of skills in a single person (the pastor) that the church's ministry is enacted. Rather, it is through the collective efforts of lay and clergy that Christ is served through the ministries of the church.

CHAPTER 2

Who Are Clergy?

An Exploration of the Personality and Characteristics of Ministers

THE INTRODUCTION NOTED the varieties of ministerial personalities. Chapter 1 noted a wide variety of ministerial tasks requiring a diversity of skills. In this chapter I explore the nature of those who are pastors of local churches.

An exploration of ministerial interests, attitudes, and personhood must first posit a disclaimer: *There is no such thing as a ministerial mold from which all clergy are produced.* This must be established at the outset for clergy who will find errors and omissions as they read these words ("That is not me!"). Lay people might conclude that their pastors are, as they suspected, atypical ("Our minister is not like that!"). Both deviations may be quite correct, for there is simply no standard or norm for people in the ministerial profession. The gender, age, and race categories cited in the Introduction are correct. A variety of people are engaged in pastoral work.

Is it so obvious as to be trite to say first that clergy are human beings? Of course, they are. But when clergy function in a profession that has religious images of who they are, the image may be stronger than the reality. In the cliché "man of God," the "of God" may be stronger than the "man" (or the "woman"). In short, there is often a double-vision perception of who clergy are.

The mediating personality tends to position itself and function between contending forces.

Recognizing individual variations and perceptions of personhood clouded by images, nonetheless in this chapter I want to probe some common characteristics that are likely to be found in pastoral people. For instance, James Dittes* of Yale Divinity School discovered a common characteristic among many clergy. They are what Dittes called "mediating personalities." By that he meant that in social relationships, clergy tend to be comfortable as middlemen (or women), playing brokerage roles between contending and conflicting power groups. To illustrate the point, his research found that in adolescence, clergy would have been more likely to be in student government than in the camera club. Student government and the camera club are different types of social organizations. A camera club is a peer organization; it comprises people of similar interest working together on a common pursuit. Student government is a buffer organization. It stands between student interests and the authority structure of the school. People in student government are mediators between the student body and the governance of the whole school. Dittes claimed that people who are accustomed to brokerage roles between groups are comfortable in ministerial work. (Incidentally, they may be comfortable in other vocations requiring mediating skills. Also, people who were not active in student government are not excluded from pastoral work.)

*James E. Dittes, *Minister on the Spot* (New York: The Pilgrim Press, 1970).

The pastor of a local church is most certainly a mediator. Mediation takes place theologically between God and humanity. It takes place socially between the local church and other churches and the larger social communities. It takes place ecclesiastically as the differing age and interest groups within the church contend for places within the institution. It takes place individually, as between parent and child or husband and wife. So, then, it is not surprising that people with mediating personalities will find their way into work requiring mediating skills.

Before leaving the Dittes study, several other findings might be mentioned in this exploration of ministerial personality. Dittes found a high percentage of clergy were firstborn children in their family of origin. Much has been written about the child's position in his or her family shaping the child's, and subsequently the adult's, personality or orientation to life. First children are called "little adults." By virtue of their position among siblings, they tend to have adult responsibility thrust on them. If the parent wants something from the store, the parent tends to select the oldest child, gives him or her the instructions and the money, and trusts him or her to perform the task. Eldest children learn early to function in the adult world. Pastors of local churches tend to have that same "little adult" status in the social relationships of the congregation. They tend to "take charge" or be responsible for the larger group; they are comfortable in protecting the interest and well-being of their organization. (Again, these are general characteristics and tendencies. Firstborn children are comfortable in many other vocations. Children in other family positions are comfortable in the pastorate too.)

Dittes also found that clergy tend to prefer individual athletic games to team sports. They prefer golf and tennis to football and basketball. At first, that finding sounds incongruous to ministerial work; after all, ministers are team members of the church. However, the characteristic identified here is self-accountability. Clergy personalities tend to be those that are responsible for their own actions. They may or may not be cooperative with others in accomplishing tasks. In the pursuit of a task they will evaluate their own performance and accept the consequences of that performance.

The Dittes findings are suggestive and not prescriptive. The words "tendency to" are key. The findings do suggest an explanation of a phenomenon you may have noticed: ministers whose parents were ministers. Clergy often observe family traditions, children following the vocation of their parents. One possible explanation for that phenomenon is familial characteristics of personality.

> *For clergy personalities, wholistic is an important concept, a way of looking at the nature of all things.*

Back to the nature of the mediating personality: People who are comfortable in the middle of contending groups hold a larger view of the scheme of things. They tend to see others and life not in isolated, unrelated fragments, but as indispensable parts of the whole. Inclusive is a good word to describe this perception of the nature of things. Mediating personalities tend to have a theology of inclusiveness: God is God of the whole human family; the church is one despite its differing manifestations; people are to live together in harmony and concord. Similarly, mediating personalities are most uncomfortable when divisions are not bridged; when clan or tribe asserts a superiority over other clans or tribes; when the musicians of a local church war on the educators; when the Christians laud it over the Jews. Mediating personalities need to learn that conflict is a process of change and growth—not violence-to-the-death conflict, but conflict that seeks accommodation, the give-and-take of interpersonal exchange.

Clergy people have other personality tendencies. A potentially negative personality tendency held by many clergy is that of dependency. In its unhealthiest, most virulent form, clergy dependency latches on to the church for all its succor, support, and sustenance. It may exclude familial and peer sources of support. In many ways the church accepts and encourages such dependency. It is sometimes disguised as "faithfulness" or "commitment." Churches like that and so do clergy. The dependent pastor often finds it necessary to manipulate the church to her own ends during her active ministry. The dependent minister in retirement is almost always unhappy, for he has lost his primary source of support and meaning. Clergy and laity are cautioned not to take this tendency to its extreme. Every person is dependent on something in the normal course of life. As with most human characteristics, what is alarming is an excess of habits and attitudes that cannot be challenged or altered.

> *Churches sometimes baptize personality compulsions of the clergy as saintly virtues.*

Howard Clinebell of the School of Theology at Claremont, California, a pastor to pastors, observed that "clergy tend to have a high pleasure anxiety and a high work addiction." In chapter 1 it was mentioned that one of the images that lay people have of clergy is that they are busy. It was noted that clergy like that image and allow it to persist. Here I would note that churches like that image too. They want their pastors to be involved, to be active, to be busy. Neither lay nor clergy conceive of this as sin: It is the name of the game.

There is nothing inherently sinful about being involved, active, and busy—except in excess. The Clinebell quotation states the excess. Some clergy are workaholics. (Chapter 4, on "The Care and Feeding of Clergy," contains an explanation of why this is often true.) For now, let it be noted that in church shorthand, workaholics are called "faithful." In the name of faithfulness, clergy families suffer; in the name of faithfulness, lay people develop unhealthy dependencies on clergy; in the name of faithfulness, clergy can become tyrants of local churches, overseeing everything from the turning off of lights to the ordering of candles.

Without meaning to, churches exploit the work addictions of clergy personalities. In the absence of clarity about their sphere of responsibility, lay people let clergy take responsibility for the whole church. When done according to the wishes of the laity for their church, it is a virtue; when done to the contrary, it is a source of complaint. Either way, it is a vice made virtuous. When it comes to church work, clergy rarely say no; it goes against the ministerial, workaholic personality to say so.

Clergy, like all other people, have struggles with compulsions. A compulsion is an irresistible drive to achieve certain objectives, often at the price of causing pain and sorrow for themselves and others. Some clergy, like some human beings, have compulsions for alcohol, sex, money, and power. All human beings have to come to grips with those drives within themselves. Stated positively, they are some of the basic forces of life that makes us strive for achievement, acceptance, satisfaction. They are problems when they become pathological, pursued beyond reason, becoming self-destructive. Pathological drives require professional counseling. An alcoholic minister should be treated with the same care and concern as any other alcoholic. So, too, with those who are compulsive about sex or money. Pathological behavior must not go unchallenged, and people and institutions affected adversely must be protected from the pathology of these drives, while at the same time the person should be protected from self-destructive behavior by corrective therapies.

It is probably not so, but there seem to be trends in clergy pathology. Whatever surfaces in the culture as collective problems of excess—alcoholism, for instance—tends to become the common affliction of clergy as well. Recently, social attitudes toward divorce have tempered. It used to be that a divorced clergy was ostracized from church and profession. Right or wrong, this is not as true today. By and large, neither the church nor the profession seems to have suffered by the presence of divorced clergy.

In understanding clergy compulsive behavior, lay people may be helped by differentiating between episodes and patterns. Episodes do not have durations or habitual characteristics. But a pattern involves repeated behavior that is destructive to the person herself or himself or to others.

Human sexuality is a perennial problem among clergy. This is not new. Historically, celibate popes had illegitimate children. Changing social mores affect us all, including clergy. Without being moralistic about it, clergy should know that when their whole professional effectiveness rests on congregational trust, any incident of untrustworthiness affects that pastor/parish relationship. Lay people should know that clergy have unusual temptations. They are, after all, lovers of people. They are involved daily in intimate relationships with parishioners. The circumstances for indiscretion are ever present. Given the circumstances of an unmet need in the clergy and a vulnerable parishioner, a mutual relationship may develop. Healthy self-images on the part of clergy and lay people are the only reliable antidotes to circumstantial opportunities.

> *In matters considered breaches of moral rectitude, the differentiation between episodes and patterns is helpful.*

Clergy suspected or confirmed in moral lapses are serious problems for churches. The complexities of Christian morality are never more visible than when they center on pastoral misconduct. Moral judgmentalism and legalism abound in such circumstances. A clergy involved in adultery is a clergy about to become controversial. Never mind that Jesus invited the accusers of adulterers who were themselves free from sin to cast the first stone. When Jesus laid those conditions on ostracism, only a pile of unused stones remained. So, the dilemma of standing for something and of forgiving the sinner is rampant in situations of clergy misconduct.

What can one say to a congregation that is struggling with a casebook study of Christian morality? In such instances congregations should be counseled to prioritize repentance and forgiveness. This is Step One in Christian morality. There is a Catch-22 to that application of Christian morality: Genuine repentance and forgiveness are always followed by resurrection. Have the people forgiven and repentant come to a newer, fuller life through repentance and forgiveness? That is the test. Whether or not resurrection follows is the indicator of an episode or a pattern.

If a congregation finds no sign of resurrection, then Step Two is "loving the sinner while hating the sin." Demand professional therapy for the clergy in the genuine effort to preserve himself or herself from harmful repetition.

Step Three, allowable only after Step One and Step Two, is dismissal. Enter Step Three gravely, but do so in the knowledge that free human beings must be accountable for their actions. A human being is free to do as he or she chooses, but a human being is not free to avoid the consequences of his or her choices.

The preceding counsel is offered in fear and trembling. Moral accusations are never clean and clear. There are always two sides to every accusation of immorality. Churches, even more than society, have been warned about hypocrisy. Hypocrisy is judgment without grace. Congregations should know that clergy are highly vulnerable. They are easily accused of misconduct. Further, they are not well protected. Most denominations do not have a court of adjudication or a system for admitting evidence, not even a process of coping with allegations. Hearsay and undocumented allegations run rampant in clergy accusations. When the trust level is near zero, trumped up charges abound and false accusations fly. In the absence of due process, clergy and laity alike are wisely counseled to avoid the situation. In the vernacular, keep the lid on allegations of clergy immoralities. In public they will be a whirlwind and your church will reap the wild wind.

Always consult with denominational officials in these matters.

In clergy relationships, too, the ounce of prevention is more valuable than tons of cure.

The preceding advice to churches is next to worthless and offered only because the expression of guidelines helps one to know where one deviated from them. The subsequent advice to congregations, however, is priceless. This is advice on how to understand the ministerial personality.

Clergy are people oriented. They have personalities that would rather be with people than with things or numbers. This is not to say that things or numbers escape their attention or interest; it just says that their primary orientation is to people. In the science of management there is an inventory, the Likert Inventory,* that examines the relationship between people concerns and task concerns. The most effective executive is one whose people and task concerns are equal. Clergy, as leaders of institutions, should be like good executives, with equality betwen people and task concerns—and some clergy are. But the tendency of most clergy is to be disproportionate in favor of people above task. A parishioner crisis will almost always take precedent over sermon preparation. A congregation may not be especially sensitive to this personality trait of their pastor. They hear a half-baked sermon on Sunday and assume that their pastor is half-baked, not that the pastor allowed a people matter to supersede his or her task.

Derived from their mediating personalities, clergy tend to perceive the church's lay constituency in groups. They see young/old, musician/missionary, attender/disciple, cantankerous/cooperative, etc. This is a professional necessity. The danger, of course, is in pigeonholing people. Many a minister is surprised to discover that the older members of the congregation want their pastor to spend a lot of time with young people. But ever the mediator, clergy want each and every group to accord all other groups equal status and virtue. Clergy tensions rise when this does not happen. The primary stress in a pastor's soul is the stress of conflicting groups within a church. It violates his or her perception of the wholeness of all things and condemns his or her preferred mediating role. Unresolved group conflict in the church is a drain on clergy energy, a cause of burnout or weariness in clergy. The stress is related to the ministerial personality that sees itself as the mediator between groups.

---

*Rensis Likert, *The Human Organization: Its Management and Value* (New York: McGraw-Hill, 1967).

Thus, ministerial personality profiles include a tendency toward mediation, work addiction, and the service of people individually and in groups. Far from being paragons of virtue, clergy, like others, have their compulsions and even self-destructive pathologies.

In that summary of personality tendencies, it should emerge that clergy persons are not much different than any other human person. In their humanness they deserve the same understanding and care as any other person. But one cannot complete a clergy personality profile without an exploration of the religious and spiritual components in the pastor's personality.

This exploration of the pastor's religion begins with the same disclaimer that was made about the human personality: There are all kinds and not one is a standard or a norm by which all others are judged, evaluated, or understood. Simply put, there is great variation in the religion of pastors.

The religious faith of those who are pastors is complicated to explain. Only some general descriptive phrases can be offered here. Because lay people assume that pastors have religious faith, they rarely ask pastors to converse about the specifics of their faith. Pastors and lay people need to have specific discussion about the components of their faith.

The religion of clergy is theological, meaning disciplined, historical, comprehensive, and intellectually structured.

Clergy are theologians. Most churches do not ordain a person into the ministry without theological education. Whatever else theological education is (see chapter 3 for a fuller exploration), it is an approach to religion. Clergy religion may begin with a simple credo: "I believe in God and in God's Son, Jesus Christ, as Lord and Savior." But in the process of theological education the clergy will examine that simple credo by historical standards of biblical faith and the historical expressions of that faith in the church. If one says that Jesus Christ is Lord and Savior, the next questions are lord of what and what does he save us from? These questions lead to some inquiry into the nature of humanity, the human predicament, the signs of grace. The question of the relationship between Christ and the church leads to a whole series of inquiries about the nature and purpose of the church, missions, the arts, and life together in fellowship with Christ. Without specifying the answers that these questions pose, let it be noted that the theology of the clergy has been pressed and pressed by theological education to examine and reexamine simple affirmations of belief until their religion expands to include all of life.

Clergy religion, therefore, is not a compartment of thought or a segment of life. In the clergy personality, religion becomes a world view, a way of looking at everything. An obvious implication of this theological world view is that religion becomes the highest priority because it is the key to everything else in life.

Because this is not a theological textbook I cannot delve into the merits of particular theological systems. Let it be noted, however, that there are various theological systems. Some systems, and hence some clergy, are evangelical, placing a high value on personal experience and biblical authority. Some theological systems, and hence some clergy, are liberal, meaning that they are liberated from the orthodox frameworks of the first century or the nineteenth century. In their place, liberal religion accepts contemporary ideas as a way of explaining or understanding the historic Christian faith. Some theological systems have high ecclesiology, so the clergy of these systems have high doctrines of the church, its worship, and its mission.

Many contemporary clergy's theological beliefs are an amalgam of these basic systems. Only a pastor can sort out for the local church the stance he or she takes toward these theological systems.

The religion of pastors may not be congruous with the religion of the laity. As I have been saying, clergy belief is theological, systematic, refined by years of inquiry. Sometimes the so-called progressive views of the clergy are shocking to the laity. Never mind that lay religion has infinite varieties, it is still jolting for lay people to find that their pastors do not agree with them. (Remember: Pastors may not agree with one another on matters of religion either!) In churches, respect for differing views is a greater good than agreement on all the views of religion.

It should not be shocking to lay people that faith is a personal and intellectual struggle for clergy too. In, say, forty years of ministry, clergy change their mind, change emphases, change systems. It's not surprising that the religion of clergy, like that of lay people, has peaks and valleys. The only difference is that clergy, in low points of faith, still must function as if their faith is constant. In these moments clergy feel hypocritical and guilty. It is helpful to all to remember in these peaks and valleys that God *alone* is constant; human perceptions of God rise and fall.

> *Unless religious faith is a property, clergy cannot "lose their faith."*

Experienced clergy have some inkling into the ebb and flow of faith. Sometimes faith at ebb points is circumstantial, emanating from changed circumstances in their own lives. Struggles with faith often are greater because of isolation. Clergy are reluctant to discuss faith crises with lay people. This is one reason having pastors to pastors is an important service of the denominational church. If lay people need pastors, so, too, do pastors need pastors in about the same sense.

The most healthy religious personality in pastors is a personality resting on true humility. True humility involves a measurue of skepticism and detachment about one's own faith. A clergy person is not God, only one who attempts to be a representative of God. True humility in pastors is not desiring that all others think as the pastor thinks, but that all others join the pastor in a pilgrimage in search of the ineffable mystery of God.

CHAPTER 3

How One Becomes a Minister

An Exploration of "the Call," Theological Education, and Ordination

HAVING EXPLORED THE WORK clergy do and the personality of people who are clergy, I turn now to the processes of preparation for religious leadership. In a sense, this is a perfunctory chapter illustrating the bromide that pastors are made, not born. There are definite steps taken in the process of becoming the pastor of a local church, and these are identified and discussed in this chapter. But far from being perfunctory, this chapter offers deepening insights for lay people about what clergy do and who they are. If the preceding chapters were on "what" and "who," this chapter is on "how." How does one become a pastor?

The very mention of a process for becoming a pastor suggests a mechanical procedure. Started as raw material at the beginning of an assembly line, a person emerges at the end of the line a finished product—a bright, shiny, new pastor. No process of ministerial development could be farther from the truth. There is nothing mechanical or automatic about "a process of preparation." But clergy do not just appear by spontaneous combustion in the church pulpit. They come from somewhere, are affected by something, and are able to lead. This chapter travels the middle paths between automation and spontaneous combustion.

These multiple paths of preparation are under an umbrella, a dome, a structure. That common roof is the church and what it represents: God, Jesus Christ, the Holy Spirit. These are active agents in the process of pastoral preparation.

The process for becoming a minister begins somewhere. In church shorthand the beginning point is "the call." One is called to the ministry. This is where it starts. But what does it mean to be called?

In a strict sense everyone is called. Orthodox theology asserts that in the providence of God all persons offer themselves, their talents, their all in the service of God. The butcher, the baker, the candlestick maker are all called by God to render meat, wheat, and tallow useful in God's world. So, all people are called of God to their work. How did God call some people to be homemakers, some to be accountants, some the owners of small businesses? There is nothing more mystical or magical in their calls to do what they do than the calls to pastors to do what they do.

Modern social conceptions have blurred the sense of call. Given its penchant for categorizing all things into separate and distinct compartments, one accepts a neat division of work (and hence of calling to that work) as *sacred* or *secular.* The difference, goes this popular convention, is that sacred work is God's work and secular work is the work of humanity. This convention is so bad that we should gag on its twistedness. The English language corrects our distortion. The word vocation (meaning the work of butchers, bakers, and candlestick makers or whatever) is an English word with Latin origins. The Latin word is *vocare,* meaning "to call." So, whatever the vocation, etymologically we are called.

Technically, the clergy are twice called. They are called first to be Christian. They share that with lay people. The second calling is to the service of other Christians. One can, and should, quibble over terms, but short of redefining the English language, we must make do with commonly accepted terms. So we ask, How is a minister called to the ministry?

> *The call to the ministry emerges in the consolidation of events, experiences, and persons seen retrospectively.*

Literalism is the stumbling block to the ministerial call. That is, a call literally implies a person summoning and a person responding. So, in a literal sense, a pastor called by God is one who sees visions or hears voices. One of the staples in pulpit humor is the story of the farmer who saw in the sky the letters G.P.C. The farmer was sure that that was his calling to the ministry, for the letters certainly meant "Go, preach Christ." So, he left his farm and entered the ministry, but it was a lackluster ministry, one that was mutually disappointing to him and to the congregation. Finally, one of the lay members, on hearing of their pastor's call, suggested to him that he had misread the sign. It means "Go, plow corn." The preacher returned to his agrarian life and lived happily ever after. Bad theology and bad jokes arise from literal meanings of the call of God.

Yes, it is true that Jesus had a mountaintop experience known as the transfiguration. It is also true that Saul of Tarsus was struck blind by a vision on the road to Damascus and subsequently joined the ranks of the apostles. And yes, classic and contemporary testimony abounds with events of transfiguration and transformation. These events usually come in a flash, an arrested moment in time when it all becomes clear. But neither Jesus nor Paul had much to say about those extraordinary experiences. The Bible is filled with their subsequent response and development, but little is said about the call itself. Are pastors those who, like Paul, were knocked off their donkeys by God's call? Some were, but not most.

Must a call be instantaneous? Must it be a once and only experience? Must it result in such illumination that everything is seen in astonishing clarity? Maybe. And maybe not. Suppose the call is metaphorical and not literal. It has the same characteristics in metaphor as literally: a change in direction, an increased awareness of self and purpose, an expression of commitment to the service of God. Couldn't the metaphor appear over a series of days, years, decades? Is there any reason a call must be instantaneous and not in a consecutive series?

If a call is metaphorical and reappears in the consecutive sense, then there is a criterion for discerning the call of God in one's life: It is the criterion of retrospect. As one looks back over the circumstances of life from the standpoint of the present, one discerns patterns with randomness punctuated by choices. One sees personality traits. One sees early childhood and familial configurations. One sees admired and respected people that become models of what one wants to become. One sees groups that have encouraged or discouraged one.

Many contemporary pastors employ this criterion in explaining their call to the ministry. Sometimes it can be vividly documented: a mother, a pastor, a friend, a youth group. Most often the documentation is general, not specific. They had feelings, thoughts, and experiences. Is that a call? In unofficial ways they "checked it out." Everyone does this, tending to erase from memory those tests that were negative.

If you accept this assertion that the call to the ministry is metaphorical and discernible in retrospect, then consider the possibility that the call to the ministry is an ongoing possibility, a continuous process. Its emergence is most often associated with young adulthood, when young men and young women sort out who they are and what they want to become. But really, it is a lifelong process. Some people have a call to the ministry later in life. Some pastors, later in life, are called to the selling of insurance, or whatever, and leave their pastorates.

Such instances of revisions in the call are part of a larger social phenomenon. People change careers with relative ease in this society. There is much wisdom in the protest "What right has a twenty-two-year-old kid to decide what a fifty-four-year-old will do with his or her life?"

To be sure, the call to the ministry involves a heightened sense of God-consciousness. In piety, one may want to say, "The great, holy God laid a hand on my shoulder and turned me toward the ministry." More likely, it was not a divine intrusion. That is always there. Rather, it was a response to the wonderings and longings of life that made the presence and power of God vivid and real. For these impious reasons, people should be encouraged by their friends and colleagues to enter the ministry. Too often, recruitment for the ministry is seen as God's task, God's laying on of hands, and we mortals should not interfere. Nonsense. In theological language the call of God is mediated—mediated through others. Why not you? It should be becoming clear that the ministry is no hiding place, no safe refuge from the vexations of the world. Not every person can or should be recruited for the ministry, but that is a different issue. Fitness for the ministry is between God and the minister.

The most important aspect of the call to the ministry is not the call itself, but the response to it.

If the path to the ministry begins with a call—literal or metaphorical, instantaneous or sequential, checked out and mediated—the validation of that call is tested by a process of preparation. The next step in becoming a minister is a time of preparation. When Paul had that transforming experience on the road to Damascus, the first thing he did not do was head for the nearest church. Rather, he went away for a time of preparation.

Every denomination requires some sort of preparation for religious leadership. The process of preparation can be placed in the midst of extremities. On the one hand, a minister can have a strong personal call to ministry. That minister can set up his or her own church and be its pastor. Inevitably, that church would become the extension of the minister and his or her personal faith. Such religious bodies are best known as sects. In a free society sects abound. There is a measure of unctuousness about such sects; they claim that God has created their "true" church. In fact, it is the charismatic leader who has done the creating, and allegiance to the leader's views is the cohesion of the sect.

On the other hand, a form of protectionism can be fostered by the preparatory period. It is exclusionary, keeping out certain undesirable types by requiring them to first demonstrate their acceptability. Acceptable to whom? Acceptable to the powers that control churches.

The preparation for ministry in mainline Protestantism is neither toward laissez-faire charisma nor crass exclusionism, although it may stray toward either extremity. The typical process for Protestant clergy is three years of graduate study in a theological seminary. This is the second step in the process of preparation, the appropriate next step in testing out the validity of one's call to the ministry.

Theological education is an important factor in the process by which one becomes a clergy person, so it must be discussed as a way of understanding clergy. It is worrisome to lay people that theological education is confused and confusing. Many lay grievances are aimed at the seminary. "They don't teach them how to preach!" is a favorite barb. The truthful answer is, "Yes, they do, and no, they don't." Such convoluted answers often add to the sense of confusion about theological education by the laity.

> *Theological education is the study of God, but how do you study a mystery?*

Back up. Before lay people become critical about the finished products coming from seminaries, let them consider the role of a seminary. Begin with its position. A theological seminary is in the middle of two powerful entities: the church and higher education. Because there is no other entity so positioned, there is nothing else like a seminary. It is a unique school.

Its church relatedness is obvious. Seminaries exist because churches want them. They pay for them. They turn to them. They have made theological education a prerequisite for ordination. In one sense, seminaries and churches have a partnership about the nature of religious leadership. They have a constantly reexamined contract about what constitutes effective leadership for the contemporary church. As church and society have become more complex, so has the contract between the churches and the seminaries. Also, different kinds of churches require different kinds of seminaries. Some seminaries are evangelical, some liberal, some ecclesiastical. Most are an amalgam of those and more. This is part of the confusion.

Lay people should know that not all institutions of religion and education are the same. For instance, a "Bible college" is not the same institution as a mainline Protestant seminary. The curriculum, the assumptions, the process are quite different. Most churches of mainline denominations do well to have pastors who are educated at mainline Protestant seminaries. This is not an iron-clad guarantee, but much havoc has been wrought by its breach.

A seminary is also an institution of higher education. It is accredited, meaning that its curriculum, its library, its faculty, and so on are reviewed. Some seminaries are literally part of a major university. Their academic standards are set by the university itself. But whether or not the seminary is a division of the university, it is an institution of higher education, preserving and extending standards of scholarship, teaching accepted methods of inquiry and discussion.

There is a constant struggle in seminaries between these two forces; seminaries bend back and forth between the two forces. Sometimes they tilt to the side of producing ministerial technicians; sometimes they tilt toward the side of producing academicians who are unfamiliar with the ways of a church. In a curious way, the truth is that if a seminary is confused, tilting back and forth, ever trying to do old things in new ways, it is probably doing its job.

Historically, the purpose of a seminary was to provide a learned clergy. In past times clergy were often the most educated people in town, not only preaching in churches, but also teaching in schools and bringing culture to the community. Today an American town has a cultural heritage because yesterday a learned clergy brought religion and culture to that community. Today a theological seminary has a slightly different focus. Today the primary purpose of a seminary is to engage in, establish, and promote the theological method of inquiry and research.

Notice, this is not the same thing as preparing people to be pastors of local churches. Yes, theological education is a means for people to test their call to the ministry, but this is not all a seminary is and does.

Like a college, a seminary is a community of scholars. Students and faculty share a quest for the nature of religion and the sharing of a religious life. But the seminary is also like a university, in which pioneering research is done. Scholarship is the tool of theology, and a theologian must learn to use the tools of inquiry and affirmation. The seminary is like a church, having a purpose outside itself and its self-perpetuation. The purpose of a seminary is to serve Christ and the church through intellectual disciplines.

In the process of three years of graduate study at an accredited seminary, a student is expected to master basic theological disciplines. He or she should graduate knowing how to think theologically and how to continue his or her growth through a lifetime of leadership and service. Not surprisingly, there is no surefire way to learn to think theologically. There are a few time-tested approaches that, when mastered, help one to learn the theological disciplines of intellectual research and communication. They are:

1. *The study of the holy scriptures.* A student in a theological seminary will study the Bible. It is one thing to read the scriptures as devotional material; it is another altogether to read the Bible as a textbook, a casebook, a lab book. In the seminary the Bible is read with a ruthless quest for truth. "It ain't necessarily so," sang Sportin' Life in *Porgy and Bess.* Seminarians learn the critical method of Bible study. Such a method supposes that the historical environment, the original languages, and the theology of *that* time are pertinent to the meaning of biblical texts. Theories abound and competent scholars argue with one another about the strengths of their theories and the weaknesses of others'. Seminarians enter this volatile world of scholarly inquiry into scripture. Yes, like Sportin' Life said, sometimes simple faith in things as they seem "ain't necessarily so." The truth is the intended end of the

theological method. Usually, the scholarly inquiries result in a discovery of new truth, which leads to a new, confident faith.

2. *Church history.* The institutional church, like its pastor, did not appear by spontaneous combustion. The church came from somewhere, serving some purpose, bearing some heritage. Church history asks where the church came from, why it exists, and what it is striving to become.

For those with deepening theological understandings, the Bible is a church history textbook—first the people of Israel and then the covenant community of early Christianity. And still later, someone had to decide what books were in the Christian Bible. It was the church that decided what the Bible was. This knowledge is related to the early period of church history. Through the centuries the church's story goes on. Is one qualified to be a Protestant pastor without some refined and vital understanding of the issues of the Reformation? Much romanticism and myth abound about the life of the church in earlier eras. Most contemporary lay people are sure that there once was a time when the Christian life and the Christian faith were simpler, purer, stronger than they are now. Students of church history know that it never was so. Christianity was always complicated and there is little in the contemporary church that is without historical precedent.

Is church history just miscellaneous information about bizarre circumstances in the past? Not at all! It is crucial information to those who aspire to be religious leaders of local churches today. The church has been around a long time. In the process it has learned how to impact its society, to preserve its traditions, and, yes, how to adapt to changing circumstances. This institution that lay and clergy share and serve is not a fragile reed destined for the dust heap of history, unraveling if we make mistakes.

Church historians are familiar with the tenacity and the vulnerabilities of the church. This is relevant knowledge.

3. *Historic and constructive theology.* It may be shocking to learn that you are not the first person in the world to ask what a human being is, where this world is going, what is the good life, or what is the meaning of human existence. These questions have been asked over and over. The questions and their answers are in the rich depository of Christian theology. The Bible raises those questions and so does the historic church. A seminarian studies the recorded works (as well as the life and times) of theologians. The inquiry may become very erudite and sophisticated—how did Thomas Aquinas rely on Aristotle's philosophy? How did Martin Luther interpret Paul? How does the Copernican revolution affect the creation stories of Genesis, and what of the findings of Darwin? In historical theology those questions have flamed across human intellect. Theology rarely invents the wheel; it builds on what is known about locomotion and creates a vehicle for today.

Constructive theology is the process in which the enduring questions of God and humans are addressed in comprehensive, cohesive thoughts relevant to contemporary understandings. They may be cosmological, arising from the findings of astronomy; they may be anthropological, arising from the insights of the humanistic sciences; they may be philosophical, arising from new approaches to philosophy. A seminarian attempts to create and articulate—and defend—a comprehensive faith statement.

Learning the theological method is crucial for Protestant pastors, for what is the contemporary church if it is not an institution struggling to know, to cope with, and to find meaning in the totality of life?

Theological education claims that theology is the queen of the sciences. If one believes in the reality of God, the divine presence in all and through all, then there is no area of inquiry that is not an inquiry into the existence and manifestation of God. Some may be dismayed that theological education takes what is simple and makes it complex. Hold your dismay, for the apparent complexity is the systematic attempt to discover the presence of God in all that is. Sure, that too is pertinent knowledge for pastors. The true end of theological education is not the boastful assertion of knowledge gained by these extensive and intensive inquiries; rather, the intended end of theological education is humility at the discovery of the vastness of God.

Virtually every mainline Protestant seminary requires its students to exhibit a mastery of those three disciplines. They are the basic tools of the theologian. They will be perfected and used for a lifetime. Only the seminary, uniquely positioned between the church and higher education, can begin the process of acquiring and using those tools for oneself.

But there is more to the theological curriculum. The following may or may not be present in a particular seminary.

4. *Religion and psychology.* Most seminary curricula include courses in religion and psychology. This is a legitimate exploration for seminarians, for it probes the questions of human nature. Who are we? Why do we do what we do? What is normal behavior? How do we cope with the stresses of life? Usually, such courses have two dimensions. First, there is an acquaintance with contemporary psychological theory. Then, there are clinical courses in which seminarians meet clients in one-to-one relationships under the practiced eye of experienced clinicians. Such clinical courses may be held in a hospital under the supervision of a certified hospital chaplain. Invariably, these courses provoke an intense introspection on the part of the students. They also establish professional proce-

dures of what a person can and cannot do in pastoral counseling.

Incidentally, there is often a dialogical exchange in these disciplines, as more and more humanistic psychologists are discovering the healing and therapeutic powers of religion in disordered lives. So, the seminary itself is a frontier in which theologian and psychologist meet to share their research and theory about human behavior.

5. *Ethics and the social sciences.* Most seminaries offer courses in the study of humanity in a social context. Like courses in religion and psychology, such courses have both theoretical and clinical dimensions. The issues of what a good society is, what a Christian society is, are explored in this discipline. Subspecialties of inquiry often attract a student's particular interest. These may be in the area of family studies, or aging, or the status of minorities. Sometimes seminarians explore such pioneering subjects as biomedical ethics, which deals with things like the implications of genetic tampering and euthanasia. Here again, there is intellectual dialogue with science or philosophy. An acquaintance with the vocabulary and literature of the social sciences is relevant to theological education, for it points toward the ways in which institutions function in an increasingly urbanized and complex society.

6. *Religion and art.* With varying degrees of intensity and intentionality, seminaries offer courses in the arts, ranging from music and theater, to dance and the visual arts, through literature and architecture. There is no doubt about the strong presence of the arts in the Christian tradition. Much of the great art in Western civilization has biblical or theological subjects or themes. Some uncertainty exists about the place of the arts in the theological curriculum. Often exposure to the arts is informal and optional, such as singing in a seminary choir or touring art

museums in metropolitan areas. Some seminaries have found it possible for their curricula to include work with some of the communication arts, such as television or film.

The lay reader may have noticed that contemporary Protestantism is not as vital as it should be in supporting and expressing faith in artistic forms. This is due, in part, to the limitations in the resources of the seminaries fully to embrace the arts in their curricular offerings.

7. *World religions.* Recognizing the shrinking of the world and the more frequent contact of global cultures, positively and negatively, the seminary curriculum usually includes some study of religious systems other than the Judeo-Christian religion. Such courses bring out the uniqueness of the Christian religion as well as increase the understandings of non-Christian cultures. An appreciation for international missions certainly requires a rudimentary understanding of world cultures. Persistent tensions in the Middle East, the taking of hostages at the embassy in Iran, and the problems of population control in India are examples of Christian concern necessitating some understanding of religions other than one's own Christianity.

These seven approaches are the major intellectual pursuits undertaken in mainline Protestant seminaries. The sketchy citation of their breadth and scope suggests to lay people both the implications for understanding pastoral competency and the strains on seminaries attempting to do such wide-ranging things with limited resources. Since the 1960s most theological education has been cooperative among seminaries. Individual seminaries are joined in clusters, or consortiums, whereby the students from one school are also eligible for courses in other schools in the cluster, thus broadening the offerings of the curriculum. One important result of that cooperation is the crossing of traditional denominational lines for theological education. A student in a United Methodist seminary may be taught by the faculty of a nearby Presbyterian or Lutheran seminary. Cooperative theological education is producing cooperation and understanding among local denominational churches.

There is one additional area of theological education to describe: the "practical curriculum." Seminaries do have a responsibility for the performing areas of pastoral ministry. This is the area in which many lay people—and clergy too—are critical of the seminary. The complaint is that seminaries do not teach ministers to preach, teach, or "run a church." In the first place, this is not so. And in the second place, there is a valid defense of the seminary in these matters.

At some point in theological education, students do take courses in preaching, Christian education, and polity, or governance of a church. These so-called practical courses *are* offered in seminary. Often too the seminary requires of the students a "field work," or clinical, experience. These are on-site learning situations. A student may work with a church during summers, on weekends, or at various times during the year while attending school. Presumably, this is simulated professional experience, much as doctors intern in a hospital. Such field work experiences are only as good as the situations allow. They are poor when a local church simply wants some cheap help; they are good when the pastor and the congregation intentionally see themselves as teachers of the seminarians. So, in curriculum and in field work the seminary does try to bridge the gap between academic course work and professional performance.

The legitimate defense of the seminaries in this regard is to point out the limitations of simulated learning. There really is no substitute for experience. Pastors finally learn to be pastors by being pastors. The simulations of the practical courses and the field work have a phoniness and a protection built into them. In terms of the first-chapter distinctions about ministerial presence and performance, these simulations never have the presence factor for the students. Further, until they have actually experienced pastoral life, most students do not even know what questions to ask or what learning is required. Thus the practical courses of the seminary can go only so far.

This is why, in this section on theological education, I must make a strong plea for continuing education. Continuing education is different than seminary education. A seminary has standards and prescribed goals; it says you must take this course and you will be graded on it. A cumulative record is kept of what you have done and how well you have done it. The accumulation determines whether or not you graduate and receive a degree. Continuing education is not like that; yet it is as vital to healthy congregations as theological education is.

Excluding the pursuit of advanced degrees, continuing education for clergy is laissez-faire. Some clergy do not do it at all; some do it haphazardly. The simplest form of continuing education is continued learning in the pastorate. Clergy begin the practice of ministry with high resolves to do just that, but within months their resolutions are broken. They allow study to become mere preparation. They fail to keep up their biblical or historical disciplines. It is a fault of clergy, but the incentives and rewards of continuing education are dropped. Not only do churches not demand it, but also they often support it only grudgingly. (The case for sabbatical and study leaves for pastors is made in later chapters.) Continuing education is the best form of education. Having served in pastorates, clergy soon come to understand what further study they need. Sometimes such study is readily available and sometimes it is not. The point here is that, given the limitations of simulation in theological curricula, when pastors are engaged in the practice of ministry, they must seek and obtain continuing education.

Before concluding this section on theological education, the lay reader may want to know more about the nomenclature of the academic degrees that pastors hold. They may see these as initials after a pastor's name on a letterhead.

Clergy educated in mainline Protestant seminaries usually have two degrees. They have a college degree, a bachelor's degree in the arts or sciences of a college, cited as an A.B., B.A., or B.S. degree. (A college degree is a normal prerequisite for admission to a seminary.) The second degree most pastors hold is a Master of Divinity, cited as an M.Div. (This degree was changed in the 1960s. Previously, it was known as a Bachelor of Divinity. Some pastors matriculating before then will cite their theological degree as a B.D.) The usual time required for these two basic degrees is seven years, four for a college degree and three for a seminary degree.

Some clergy hold advanced degrees. Some clergy hold a Doctor of Ministry, cited as a D.Min., which is an additional year of theological study, usually done after one has become a pastor. A few clergy have a Doctor of Philosophy, Ph.D., or a Doctor of Education, D.Ed. There is also an honorary degree, Doctor of Divinity, D.D. All these entitle the holders to be known as "Doctor."

Other common theological degrees are S.T.M., a Master of Sacred Theology; M.A., Master of Arts; and a Doctor of Theology, D.Th. The academic color of theological degrees emblazoned on the symbolic hood is red.

In the main, theological education is a way of testing one's call to the ministry. Does one have an aptitude and appetite for the skills required in theological education? Seminary is a kind of winnowing process. Some never complete it; some complete seminary and either stay on in seminary work or apply their theological learnings in nonpastoral work. The majority of seminarians become pastors. It is not at all clear that mastery of the theological disciplines is ipso facto proof of one's fitness for pastoral work.

In the normal sequence of preparation of how one becomes a minister, a third and decisive step is taken: ordination. When Jesus selected Peter as "the rock upon whom I will build my church" (Matthew 16:18), he laid his hand on Peter's head. In the ritual of ordination the previously ordained place their hands on the head of the ordinand and pray with him or her. This is a symbolic gesture, transferring apostolic tradition to the new clergyperson.

What does the ritual mean? The meaning depends on how a denomination views the orders of the church. If a church has two distinct orders, lay and clergy, then the ritual of ordination allows one to enter into, stand with, and perform the functions of that order in the church. Most mainline churches are not so precise about the orders of the church, but neither are they vague about ordination. It means something. It means that this person is now a minister with standing in the whole denomination. It means that this ordained person is authorized by the denomination to be a pastor of a local church.

There are differing meanings for ordination, but some meanings are commonly held in most denominations. First, ordination is a certification that this person is qualified to perform ministerial duties. Before pastors come to the "laying on of hands" ceremony, they must present themselves for examination by an appropriate panel or committee of the church. The candidate must present evidence of his or her theological education, usually in the form of a Master of Divinity degree from an accredited seminary. He or she must present affirmations on his or her behalf. These may be from a pastor, a local church, or some church-related agency. People who know the candidate, his or her character, his or her past life, come forth to share their knowledge of this person. Finally, in varying ways the candidate must present himself or herself and request ordination. This presentation may be a statement of personal belief or such other documents as reveal what he or she believes. The candidate must stand an examination of his or her presentations. Wide-ranging questions of opinion and interpretation are asked and answered by the candidate.

Having examined the credentials submitted and heard their defense, the certifying panel votes to accept or reject this person's request for ordination. Presumably, the panel's criteria used to make this decision are to protect the denomination from false doctrine or character unsuited to pastoral work.

But who really knows what that is and what this person will become? Most ordaining panels are not terribly judgmental, preferring to let the real commitment of this person emerge in God's time. They do have the authority, sometimes exercised, not to recommend a person for ordination or not to recommend until certain conditions are met. Because of the misuse of power and because of the difficulties in passing personal judgments, such panels usually limit themselves to being satisfied that the materials presented are valid and authentic. Their vote usually means that by these standards a person is certified for the work of the ministry.

A second meaning of ordination in most mainline Protestant denominations is what is called "setting apart." The phrase denotes a distinction between lay and clergy in the life of the congregation. Insofar as a mystical, grace-filled event can be institutionalized and ritualized, ordination represents the outward and visible manifestation that God has called this person to the ministry of Christ's church. Because no one really knows what God has done in the life of this person, the status of being set apart by God for ministry is an act of faith and pious hope that God has, in fact, chosen this person for ministry. So on behalf of The Ineffable God the church bears witness that, in faith, God has called this person to God's service. By ordination one becomes "a man (or woman) of God."

A third, less mystical meaning of ordination is the admission to the practice of ministry. From henceforth one will be a pastor of the church. What that means is not always clear. What is clear is that without ordination you are not a pastor. You may be a good, decent, capable person of pastoral inclinations, but without ordination you are not a pastor. In practical terms, then, this admission to the practice means that the ordinand is now authorized to accept a pastorate. In this sense, it is the rite of passage, of entrance.

Still further at the vocational level, ordination means entitlement to certain pastoral prerogatives. In some denominations this may mean assignment to a pastorate. (The United Methodist Church, for example, guarantees every ordinand a pastoral placement.) It may mean eligibility for participation in a denominational pension or insurance program. Ordination also establishes a legal status under certain provisions of federal or state adjudication. An ordained minister, for example, can legally perform weddings. He or she may have the option of participating in the social security system or not. In such matters ordination is the conferring of a professional status on a person with the rights and duties that apply.

In most Protestant denominations, ordination means that one is entitled to preach the Word and administer the sacraments. In the nomenclature of this book, ordination confers on a person the right and obligation to pursue the ministerial presence and performance. The sign and symbol of this meaning is usually expressed in the title conferred on one by ordination. After ordination, one is addressed "The Reverend" or "Pastor." In church shorthand, these titles mean that the clergy person has been ordained.

Ordination, the concluding stage of preparation, can be described in terms of ritual (the laying on of hands) and ecclesiastical rite (the conference of a status conforming to the orders of the church) but not so easily described is its mystical meaning. The earthly church with its laity and clergy do what they do in ordination through faith in God. Most Protestants would agree that only God ordains; everything else is representative of God's power and authority in the church. This Divine ordination is an ineffable mystery. It is between the person and God. The church would like to hope that all ordinations are at the bidding of God and pleasing to God, but the church knows God reserves the right of final judgment about the authenticity of any ordination.

Many Protestant churches have a theological way of expressing the authority of The Divine in ordination. Such churches employ the word covenant to express The Divine dynamic in ordination. The ordinand, stating vows, makes a covenant with God through the church. The covenant may be kept through all circumstances by God and the ordinand, or it may be renounced. The dynamic of the covenant is that it establishes a status at the outset but leaves to God's power its future development. In this way, ordination is both a once-and-for-all event and a continuing process.

Once one is ordained, can one be disordained? Yes, according to denominational procedures. In some denominations a pastor may demit, meaning that he or she renounces the vows of ordination and is no longer constrained by them. The church may also disordain. The word for this is defrock. Following denominational systems of adjudication, an ordained person may be disordained from the ministry by action of the authorized church body. Neither happens very often, and when they do they are the source of great sorrow, consternation, and controversy. Both pastors and churches recognize disordination as a final condition, with many preferable steps in between. That which the church gives, it can also take away.

Has this been a perfunctory chapter? At the outset it was noted that this chapter would describe the steps in the process by which one becomes a minister. Thus the call, theological education, and ordination were explored. But at the outset my intention also was to offer additional understandings of who pastors are and what they do.

The learnings worth retaining here are that no pastor merely arrives in the pulpit; each pastor is a story and has a story to tell about a long pilgrimage. Each pastor has become more, much more, than he or she once was. Each one has been seen, touched, and influenced by countless people. Maybe the pastor wants to be like his or her parents, his or her seminary teacher. Maybe he or she secretly measures his or her standards by others. Maybe he or she has a strong sense of needing to give back to other people much that others gave to him or to her. Maybe the pastor feels shortchanged by the process or perhaps overwhelmed by it all. Maybe he or she still wonders whether God called. Maybe he or she wonders whether God has had a change of mind. Maybe he or she sees the whole unfolding of the process as moments of grace in his or her life.

It might be interesting for the lay people to know about the specific process that brought their pastor to the church and to them.

CHAPTER 4

The Care and Feeding of Clergy

An Exploration of What Ministers Expect from Their Work

IN THIS CHAPTER the tone and style shift. Explorations of what clergy do, who they are, and how they become clergy have a measure of objectivity. These elements of understanding, admittedly diverse, still encompass a certain body of factual information. In medical terminology, the first three chapters are "case histories," affording, as they do, a pattern of background understandings.

This chapter and those that follow become more diagnostic and prescriptive of necessity; the tone becomes more opinionated and subjective. The problem of describing, in general terms, specific instances grows greater. Every local church, every pastor, all have unique profiles, traditions, attitudes, perspectives, and expectations. The intended purpose of broadening understandings is ever interrupted by the "Yes, but in our particular case . . ." interjection. This book both acknowledges the legitimacy of those interruptions and encourages their formation.

Given those limitations, I offer guidelines pertaining to clergy expectations. The guidelines are prescriptive, aimed at treating symptoms. The primary value of offering prescriptive guidelines is that they afford pastor and laity a focus for discussion. Also, such guidelines become standards so that clergy and lay people have a clearer sense of where, by choice or miscalculation, they changed the prescription.

Even in diagnosis and prescription, the focus remains constant: These are observations about clergy aimed at lay people intending to increase lay understanding of clergy. As such, they become words of advocacy for the clergy. Constant, too, is the focus on healthy pastor/parish relationships. The presupposition here is mutually high trust levels. These guidelines are for laity and clergy desiring to maintain and further their healthy relationship. It would be a matter of sorrow and dismay if these guidelines were to become sources of division and disease in a congregation. Their purpose is to avoid debilitating circumstances, not create them!

> *It is both demeaning and enlightening to examine pastoral work as a job, much like any other job.*

Let these observations of clergy expectations begin with a perspective. This is a view understood by most clergy and few lay people. The perspective is that of the ministry as a career.

The perception of the ministry as a career is visually enhanced by the imaginary depiction of horizontal and vertical lines. The horizontal line represents the familiar way in which lay people perceive the clergy. The horizontal line represents a pastor serving a local church. The important elements of life and work are on that horizontal line. Personal satisfactions, in terms of self-fulfillment, self-satisfaction, self-esteem, are on that horizontal line, fulfilling the needs of clergy for identity, purpose, and useful work. Also on the horizontal line are the creature needs of every human being: financial compensation, protection from the elements, a place to be, a place to grow, and a place to serve.

The point about clergy expectations suggested by this horizontal line is that the circumstances surrounding employment in a local church are only part of total clergy expectations. That is the part lay people recognize, support, and attend to. They best understand clergy expectations on the horizontal line of employment in a local church. Lay people earnestly intend to be good employers. They offer fiscal compensation, personal respect, and a genuine caring for their pastor's well-being in their community. However, not all ministerial expectations of being employed in a pastorate are circumscribed by that horizontal dimension.

An imaginary vertical line must intersect the horizontal plane. The vertical line represents a career pattern. It represents, chronologically, a career of forty years in the ministry. A career has identifiable stages. To illustrate, take the extremities: A career begins at some point in time and ends at some point in time. Ordination and retirement are the initiating and terminating words of a ministerial career. Clergy live in that vertical time line of a career too. Lay people know that vertical line is there, but it does not have the reality for them that it has for clergy.

The subsequent point to be made about these horizontal and vertical lines is that the fullest understanding of clergy requires attention to the necessities of both. Before that fuller understanding is developed, pause to consider an implication, a dramatic implication, of the horizontal and vertical dimensions in clergy work. On the horizontal line, the pastor of a congregation may (or may not for reasons I will explore later) live in a parsonage or manse. The church-owned house is provided for the pastor and his or her family *as long as he or she is in the pastorate of that church.* When the pastor dies, is disabled, or retires, what claim has the pastor on that parsonage? This is a dramatic illustration of the dimensions of the horizontal line of employment and the vertical line of a career. The subsequent analysis is that almost everything in the ministerial vocation is geared to the horizontal, with little or no attention to the vertical.

The tensions of the horizontal and the vertical produce other phenomena. Clergy move from one pastorate to another. In the imaginary depiction of the vertical and the horizontal, the vertical line will be intersected by a series of horizontal lines, representing the several pastorates served during a career. In a forty-year career, there may be three to twelve horizontal lines. Lay people understand and expect itinerant pastors. What lay people may not appreciate is what moving means in terms of the vertical career pattern.

Say that it should not be so and no one will argue, but it does exist; as long as there is a career pattern, the objective is to move "up" the vertical line. This is where the problems begin. What is "up" for clergy? How fair or unfair is it for clergy to gauge a congregation by their standards of career advancement? Decry and lament these considerations as you wish, but they will not disappear. They persist, and their persistence feeds unhealthy distortions. Such distortions must be exposed and confronted realistically.

The primary distortion resulting from career advancement is that "bigger is better." Looked at objectively and dispassionately, this is nonsense. Like all other forms of prejudice, the prejudice of size distorts the realities of what is involved in big and little.

> *It is inaccurate and invalid, but clergy tend to measure the progress of their careers by the size of the churches they serve.*

Pause a moment here to really understand why this distortion exists. It exists because so much is tied to the horizontal line. On the horizontal line, the bigger the church, the higher the salary, the greater the influence, the more challenge to competency. Therefore, because of the preeminence of the horizontal line, the evidence of career development points toward upward mobility in quest of a "bigger and better" church.

If you think this horizontal/vertical dimension is overdrawn here, just recite for yourself the number of recent seminary graduates placed as senior ministers in churches of one thousand members. The answer is not one. Why? Because the whole church knows that the proper beginning place for a pastor is in a small church. With experience, the pastor will move "up." This is the reality of the horizontal/vertical dimension.

For the benefit of clergy, it is in order to debunk the "bigger is better" myth. The truth is that *bigger is different.* Pastoral leadership in a large church is different from pastoral leadership in a small church. Large churches are complex social systems. Here is a simple distinction: The smaller the church, the more intimate the fellowship; the larger the church, the more dispersed the fellowship. Now, which is better—diverse fellowship or intimate fellowship? This question is more relevant to chew on than the assumption that bigger is better.

Lay people should understand that a very real and perplexing question for clergy is how to measure career development. Must it always be done in terms of the size of the congregation? Are there other valid indexes for career development? Lay people should try to imagine the sense of rejection—even shame—a fifty-five-year-old clergy feels when, after thirty years of service, he or she is about where he or she started.

Here's another obvious element in the career pattern

that should be exposed and confronted. In forty years of a career, persons change and their needs and interests change. Just look at the extremes for validation: Are twenty-five-year-old ministers the same as sixty-five-year-old ministers? What has happened (or not happened) to those ministers in forty years? The emphasis on the horizontal dimension exacerbates the problems of personal growth and change. A parsonage is a parsonage is a parsonage in the horizontal sense. In the vertical sense, that parsonage is too big for a twenty-five-year-old couple with no children, too small for a thirty-five-year-old family of five, and too big for a fifty-five-year-old couple. Or again, say all local churches have a policy of a three-month, paid sabbatical leave after seven years of service to the local church. After six years a pastor moves. How much sabbatical leave has that pastor received? None, because it is valid only on the horizontal. Personal changes are easily accommodated in the excesses of the horizontal dimension.

These musings on the problems of horizontal employment and vertical career patterns lead to a diagnosis. Among contemporary clergy there is an unnamed and undiscussed problem: *boredom.* Lay people will not hear of it from their pastors. Pastors will not discuss it with other pastors, lay people, or their families. Indeed, in every corner of the church it will be denied, but this diagnosis says boredom is a problem among contemporary clergy. Be clear, it is not that clergy do not have enough to do or that what they do is unimportant or unsatisfying. These are not the causes of boredom. Rather, clergy boredom is a wistful yearning, a sense that it is better somewhere else, a gnawing suspicion that "life has passed me by." How much ecclesiastical energy is dissipated by this boredom? How much unhealth festers in the envy of others, in low self-esteem, in the manipulations of congregations to allow clergy some exercise of personal power?

The preceding is a worst-case scenario. It is not being asserted that the condition of contemporary clergy is unfulfilled lives wallowing in self-pity, mired in pathetic quibbles. Far from it! The point being made here did not begin with an examination of things as they are; the point made here arose from examinations of structures affecting clergy that have destructive potential. Yes, unsavory consequences may surface from time to time, but the more common phenomenon is that they do not. Either clergy repress them or, more likely, they accept them and learn to cope with them. The absence of widespread revolt by clergy is a curious turn of affirmative truth; the strength and health of the clergy in dealing with these negative possibilities suggest a vitality bordering on robust coping power.

Presumably, a responsible author, having made a diagnosis of the existence of maladies or the horizontal/vertical dimension in pastoral life, should then offer a curative prescription. Such cure can be done, but it will not be done.

We are overchurched in terms of efficiency, but efficiency is not a great goal of the church.

The curative prescription is unpalatable, for the cure might be more painful than the disease. The horizontal and vertical patterns are related to ecclesiastical freedom. Here's what that means: In terms of efficiency, there are too many churches. Too many small churches. Too many denominations. We also have too many clergy. Mind you, this is strictly an efficiency analysis. Looked at economically, every local church is redundant to every other local church in the area. Each church has the expense of buildings, personnel, and programs. One church building with several pastoral specialists on a staff offering a wide diversity of programs in a community is much more efficient and much less expensive. If this were the norm, the problems of the vertical would be greatly diminished. (Also diminished would be many other elements of church life considered desirable.)

Consolidating churches for expediency is one prescription, but it is not offered here. Criticism of the proliferation of churches was made as a helpful standard of judgment. The real and potential unhealth of contemporary church life is the price we pay for the luxury of too many churches. Tuck this judgmental opinion in the back of your mind: Churches have sinned against God and one another by insisting on redundant institutions whose expenses might have otherwise been employed.

> *Is keeping the pastor happy a legitimate objective of local churches? No, but unhappy pastors are deterrents to other legitimate objectives of the church.*

The main theme here is that clergy expect both employment satisfactions *and* career satisfactions. Local churches engage in meeting employment satisfactions, but clergy are on their own when it comes to career satisfactions. For the most part, clergy must define for themselves what they think constitutes success, progress, growth, and the commensurate rewards attached to these achievements. For clergy, the coping with career frustrations is faith. Their faith deters them from treating their work as a job like any other job. They minimize the usual secular symbols of reward and prestige. "Faithful" is more virtuous to clergy than "successful."

Still, baptizing the phenomena of career frustrations with religion does not make the frustrations disappear. A modest palliative is to urge lay sensitivity to the career dimensions of a pastor's expectations. In the past fifty years, pension programs have become commonplace in churches. The very existence of a pension program is prima facie evidence of a career. In developing arrangements for pastors with local churches, greater care could be given to career needs. In the context of long-term compensation, churches may want to think about the implications of living for forty years in a parsonage and then, at retirement, having no home. In present plans of compensation there should be a component of future benefits pointing toward home ownership.

More satisfying to clergy, however, would be the assignment of tasks relevant to personal growth. If teaching a teenage confirmation class is not as satisfying as it used to be, then why not shift the pastor from teaching teenage confirmation to teaching an adult confirmation class as a review of the basics of faith. If the constant round of trustees' meetings is wearying to the pastor, why not commission a lay person to be the pastor's representative to the trustees for a year. These are modest alterations aimed at breaking up the routine of the regular round of pastoral work. The theory is that pacing and alteration are substitutes for stagnation in a career that seems to be going nowhere.

Lay people will not hear much complaint about the horizontal/vertical dimensions of employment and career patterns. But if lay people listen with understanding, they will hear clergy speak of a problem in their working conditions. Clergy will not come out and speak directly about these things, but clergy know they exist. Lay people should understand these peculiarities. These peculiarities are certain anomalies that come with ministerial work. These peculiar twists and ripples in clergy work are not present in the work of others. Clergy make their peace with these anomalies. The longer one is in the ministerial profession, the less one notices their presence.

Pastors work most when other people are at leisure.

For better or worse, most lay people have a structure to their lives; so do clergy, but their structure is different from others and that makes for some problems.

The structure of a week is different for clergy than for lay people. For clergy, Sunday is not a day of rest, a leisure day, a day to recoup from the week, to see one's relatives or sleep late. Sunday is the most intense work day of the week. For clergy, that's all right. It is, after all, the sabbath, and giving it one's best effort is a gesture of honor. However, here is the rub: Working Sunday throws the rest of the week into peculiar patterns. Many clergy take Monday off. Have you ever tried to do something special with your children on Monday? It never quite works out. In this day of working spouses, it is a little awkward when each has a different day off. Somehow it seems that communication is not what it should be or that the mutual satisfactions of special time together elude the two-career family.

Then there is the work week. Most people have their routines to follow Monday through Friday. So do clergy. But there is one difference. As the leaders of a voluntary organization, the clergy gather with the volunteers at *their* convenience. When is that? In the evening, of course. Clergy end up working normal daytime hours and into the evening. Sometimes they do this three and four nights a week. Lay people may say, "Well, I do that too; I'm very involved in my church and community." But for lay people, going to a church gathering is an event in their *non-work time;* for clergy, going to a church gathering in the evening is what they have been doing all day. So, clergy may work fifty to seventy hours a week.

A person with work addictions will find many satisfactions in the pastorate.

Well, one can always look forward to the holidays. Nothing much happens during the holidays and one can use these days for catch-up. That may be how it is with lay people, but not with clergy! Many holidays are religious holidays, and religious holidays are important workdays for religious leaders. Other people may look forward to the special events of Christmas and Easter, but clergy had better be prepared for a heavy load during the holidays. Not only are there additional services and programs during the holidays, but also the couple who is planning to marry in a few months will be in town and could they see the pastor? Of course, they may; pastors never say no.

What is the point of these exaggerated excerpts from the work routine of the pastor? The point is a pastoral anomaly; clergy swim upstream against the currents of life's typical patterns. Some ministerial personalities—the workaholics—thrive on this anomaly. Others just accept it as part of the uniqueness of their vocation. After doing it for years, they think little of it.

To top off this anomaly, clergy boast of "taking a day off." America went on a five-day work week in 1935. What an up-to-date and relevant profession the clergy are! They are entitled to *one* day off a week.

The real pattern, of course, is not as confining as this depiction suggests. This is another worst-case scenario. It sounds as if clergy have time for nothing but work. This is not so. They are their own bosses when it comes to managing their time. Most clergy are good about finding time away from work because they know they work more creatively when they have periods of involvement followed by periods of withdrawal. The confining problem was described in exaggeration to increase lay understanding of this anomaly.

It is my contention that the anomaly is not good for either pastors or laity. It encourages workaholism in clergy and a sense of guilt when they are not working. It encourages a dependency on the part of lay people. Lay people do not need a clergy present at every church event to make it "official." For the benefit of clergy, have you ever considered this inconsistency about excessive work? Luther's theological affirmation was "justification by faith, not works." Are the clergy living by that theology in their fifty-to-seventy-hour weeks? What are clergy justifying? And how are they justifying it? Work patterns are legitimate items for discussion and negotiation between clergy and laity. Accommodations can be found. The following guidelines are offered for discussion concerning clergy work time.

Five-day work week. Pick any five days, including Sunday, for days at work; pick any two (not Sunday) for days not to be at church. Agree that occasional circumstances—funerals, weddings, special observances—will interfere, and be glad to be available when special pastoral services are needed.

One night a week for church work. Attend the necessary committee meetings, go calling on those not reachable during the day, even write a sermon, but plan such things for one night a week only. The other six nights are free choices—for work or for leisure-time involvements.

If lay people consider that irresponsible, why not consider having all the church committees meet on the same night. Where does the Bible say that each committee is entitled to a special night with the pastor? Also, committees made up of retired lay people could meet—and might prefer to meet—during the day rather than at night.

Post-holiday holidays. Why not a week off after a holiday week? It will not be the same as having the holidays off, but if that cannot be, why not belated holidays for clergy?

One or two weeks' paid vacation every quarter, accumulative. This is fresh thinking about old patterns. In the 1930s, clergy received a month's summer vacation in lieu of forty-eight working weekends. Summer vacations are hold-overs from rural life (reinforced by patterns in public schools).

The president of a contemporary corporation argues that employees of his corporation above a certain level have no specified vacation periods. His reasoning? A person with a high level of responsibility is a person who knows the necessity of time away from the regular routines of duty. Let the person pick and choose his or her vacation periods when he or she wants and needs them, he advises. Pastors are of sufficient rank and maturity to handle that responsibly.

These advocacies are conceived in response to the anomaly of working conditions that are off center from the typical patterns of work. There is a second anomaly of clergy life that lay people should understand and meet creatively. This anomaly concerns living arrangements. The historic, and probably typical, pattern of living arrangements for clergy is the provision of a church-owned house as part of their compensation—as long as they are pastors of the church that owns the house.

The alternative to residence in a church-owned house is the provision of a housing allowance that allows clergy to purchase or rent a home of their own choice. Until recently, the housing allowance has been excluded from income tax. The interest and taxes on the mortgage and property have been tax deductible. A recent tax ruling directs clergy to compute their income tax with one benefit or the other, but not both. I contend that it is preferable for a pastor to purchase and reside in a house of his or her own choice because of the vertical career dimension.

Either way, there is an anomaly about clergy living arrangements. The anomaly is the church's expectation that the pastor will reside in the town or neighborhood in which the church is located. For some lay people, this is not surprising; in their own lives they choose to live and work in the same community. For other laity, the arrangement is odd, for they work in one place and live in another; they are commuters. A few clergy commute, too, but the usual, normative pattern is for the pastor of a church to reside near the church.

Prisoners, like pastors, have little choice about their environment, including their domicile, their companions, and the amenities of life.

Living in the community in which one works has many implications. Because the pastor lives in the community in which he or she works, he or she is immediately recognizable. Many a pastor will intend a five-minute stop in the bank and come away in a half-hour, having encountered a parishioner who wanted to discuss some personal or church matter. When you live where you work, you are never far from your work.

School systems and cultural opportunities come with the residential community. There is an unevenness about public education in the United States. More than once a pastor has decided to seek a different pastorate because his or her children deserved a better educational opportunity than the present community offered. Some clergy want to live near superior libraries, art museums, concert halls, or where there is a diversity of culture. In short, a pastor may be comfortable with a parish but uncomfortable with the community in which the church is located.

When the only housing option for the pastor is a parsonage, rectory, or manse, the living arrangements narrow still further. The housing needs of clergy vary with their age and family size; houses are not elastic, stretching or contracting to accommodate the varieties of clergy families. Further, a church-owned house is a church-managed house. There is something ludicrous about a committee meeting to decide what color to paint the bathroom! Churches are well meaning, but uneven, landlords. There is an element of paternalism in providing a place for clergy to live. It is not dissimilar to treating clergy as children, making sure they are provided for within the community.

Admittedly, there is something positive about residing in the community—and even the house—of the church. It establishes one as an involved and valued member of the community. It also helps the pastor to understand the situations and struggles of his or her parishioners. It also relieves the clergy of the hassles other families encounter in selecting a home and a community in which to reside. Then, too, a minister is a helping professional; it may be important that care be proximate to the sources of need.

Given the strong heritage of this pattern, no prescription for alternative arrangements can be offered; at least one cannot be offered that preserves the benefits while reducing the limitations. This anomaly, however, is worth citing in this section, for it has diagnostic implications that lay people should understand. Living arrangements for clergy loom larger than they should when it comes to pastoral placement. Because of the anomaly of living in the community, clergy changing pastorates have more at stake, a wider range of expectations to meet in accepting a pastoral call. It is one thing to select a church—or be selected by a church—it is something else to select a church in a community that is congenial to oneself and one's family. When the arrangements for a working spouse are added to the process, placement becomes very, very complex. Lay people should be sensitive to these complications.

The next aspect of the care and feeding of clergy is on compensation. Compensation, too, has ironical anomalies; not the least of these ironies is that lay people are more comfortable exploring these matters than clergy are. Subsequently, guidelines for compensation will be presented, but because of the discomfort of the clergy in this area, it is best to introduce the guidelines with some philosophical background.

Clergy are genuinely ambivalent about their financial compensation. Part of them would prefer that the issues did not exist. Other elements of church life are far more important than their compensation. Further, people who enter the ministerial profession have, to a certain extent, made their peace with the levels of compensation associated with the profession. In sorting out their call to the ministry, one of the elements evaluated is how important financial well-being really is to them. Usually, the accumulation of wealth is not high in their priorities. If it is, they have chosen a stupid way to pursue it.

Another part of the clergy personality acknowledges the necessity and reality of financial life. They have needs to meet, children to educate, a family to provide for. In some religious orders the clergy take a vow of poverty that they be not distracted from the pursuits of the spirit by the things of this world. The vow of poverty works best when it is linked with the vow of chastity. Protestant clergy are usually family people. One of their duties is to provide for their families. Why should a family member be penalized because of a parent's vocational traditions? In the course of a career, clergy come to realize that there is an economic necessity to life. They feel guilty and shameful when they realize that the demands of the economic order are greater than their ability to meet those demands.

A potential source of clergy unhappiness, even dysfunction, is the low pay of their profession.

The greatest inhibiting factor to clergy in matters of compensation is the multiplicity of roles. The self-interests of the clergy are in conflict with the total demands on the church budget. In their role as institutional leaders, they recognize the multiplicity of demands on and the limitation of resources of the local church. Many a pastor accepts lower compensation so that other objectives of the church may be met. Looked at crassly, the clergy themselves subsidize the church. As commendable as that is for Christian faith, it is equally deplorable for the consequences to the whole profession.

Recognizing the weight of tradition in matters of compensation, the following prescriptions for coping with patterns of low compensation may not find wide acceptance.

The first prescription is a flat-out declarative assertion: *Clergy should have higher salaries.* The assertion arises from neither the high cost of living nor the tradition of low pay. Rather, the assertion arises from a contemporary phenomenon among the profession. The profession suffers from low self-esteem. Clergy tend to think that they are not worth very much. Professional athletes, entertainers, executives are worth more than clergy—at least when compared by economic standards. Another ironic consequence of low pay is that clergy may become more materialistic, not less. They become people who count the cost of every decision they make. If the choices were luxurious frills, they could be ignored, but the choice of where to send a child to college is not a luxurious frill.

Also, the culture has a changing meaning of compensation; the culture can express approval and affection through compensation. Low salaries for clergy is a subtle form of rejection. Churches compare individual salaries of one pastor with that of other pastors. When the whole profession is underpaid, such comparisons are inadequate. So, it is simple to say: For the good of the whole profession, for the morale of its practitioners, even for the health of the whole church—clergy should have higher levels of compensation than they historically have had.

> *A church may want to key the pay scale of a pastor to a comparable position of status and responsibility in the community, say that of a high school principal.*

A second prescription about clergy compensation is conceptualization of what compensation means. This proposal wants to do away with salary in the usual sense of wages paid for services rendered. In the place of a salary, clergy should receive a stipend that enables them to reside in the community, as is expected by the congregation. Census figures on family incomes are available for every community. A church should invite a pastor to live in its community by compensating the pastor according to prevailing community standards. This guideline is acceptable to the horizontal element in pastoral expectations.

The conceptualization of clergy compensation should also involve the vertical or career dimension. Missing from the ministerial profession is a standard for compensating experience. The location, size, and circumstance of the congregation determine the level of compensation; it matters little whether the pastor has had five or thirty years of experience. The consequence of not factoring experience into clergy compensation causes widespread confusion about success and progress among the clergy. In reconciling clergy compensation along career dimensions, reconsider the parsonage question. If the clergy receive a rent-free parsonage as part of their compensation, understand the consequences of that parsonage for the clergy at the end of his or her career. It is a scandal and an affront to a valued professional career to terminate it with no place to go.

Fringe benefits are not clergy compensation; they are the costs incurred by the church in having a leader.

Great confusions abound with regard to fringe benefits. In today's world, fringe benefits have risen in cost. The rise does not alter a fact: All fringe benefits are church expenses, not clergy compensation. All fringe benefits—automobile allowance, health insurance, social security allowances, parsonage allowances, pension programs, life insurance, continuing education, and so on—should be conceived of as church expenses, like utility bills, even when they are paid directly to the pastor.

Singled out for special consideration in these guidelines for compensation are the costs of professional development. Like fringe benefits, these items are not compensation to the pastor; they are for the benefit of the church, the whole church. Because ordained ministers are required to be theologically educated and because of the complexities of their multiple tasks, clergy must have a vital program of continuing education. The prescription for this program is in two parts: annual study leave for continuing education and a periodic sabbatical leave.

A minimum of two weeks a year should be designated for continuing education. The designation should include adequate compensation to cover travel, tuition, and related costs. The time is *not* vacation time. For the good of the whole church, local congregations should demand this of their pastors.

A second aspect of professional development is the establishment of a policy of sabbatical leave. A sabbatical is a merger of religious and educational traditions. In the Bible, the word sabbath means seven. Hence, many churches, being literal, offer a sabbatical every seven years. There is nothing profound about seven; what is profound is the necessity of stepping out of and standing aloof from the regular routines for a period of refreshment and renewal. In education, a sabbatical leave is part of the scholar's life in which he or she increases his or her skills or does research on a chosen subject without the obligations of classroom duties. For clergy, the twin heritage of religious renewal and intellectual reassessments are essential to professional development.

Concluding this segment on clergy financial compensation, lay people would do well to heed this warning about a growing trend among churches. More and more parsonage families are two-income families. It is one thing to have two adults pursuing independent careers of their own choice. It is something else again to have two careers in one family because a ministerial career cannot support a family. Churches may want to look on this phenomenon as a solution to their problems: They can have full-time religious leadership with part-time costs. In the longer term, the church will suffer from this trend. If the ministry ceases to be a career, with compensation that enables full-time pursuit for a lifetime, then much of what we have come to value in the church will change.

Clergy work for pay, psychic pay.

There is one more aspect of clergy compensation, one that lay people are good about giving. That element is psychic pay. Psychic pay, in church shorthand, is "nonmaterial reward." The Bible says that a human being "does not live by bread alone." A human being does live by bread, but not bread alone. Clergy should be compensated in nonmaterial forms of pay.

This is not a plea for lay people to bite their tongues and compromise their integrity. In truth, a clergy person, just because he or she is a minister, does not deserve unqualified admiration. Some do and some do not. But it should not be withheld from those who do.

Here's why: Clergy tasks are essentially beyond measurement. Can caring be expressed in a goal? Can helping be quantified? Does inspiration have a predictable result? These may be real and knowable, but they also have indeterminable consequences. How, then, does a clergy person know what he or she has done well?

This is a major problem for ministers. They may think that they have been helpful to a parishioner, even when they have done or said what the parishioner did not want done or said. They need confirmation from the recipients of their ministry. When they have done well, tell them so.

This advocacy is more than a call to politeness, more, too, than a massage for sagging egos. Telling a pastor you appreciate him or her may be polite, but doing so has a curious and marvelous effect. Pastors are givers. All they do is give themselves, their wisdom, their faith, their skill, their care to others. When one gives and gives, the well of giving drops lower and lower. A compliment, a "thank you," an "I appreciate you," curiously, marvelously replenishes the well of giving. The truly amazing part is that when pastors know that they are appreciated, they manufacture more to give, more than they knew they had to give.

An expression of appreciation to pastors only encourages them.

CHAPTER 5

In the Beginning . . . Trust

An Exploration of How Pastoral Relationships Are Established

WHEN ANTHROPOLOGICAL RESEARCHERS enter a strange culture to learn of its ways, they know that the first few minutes will bring significant learning. The longer the researchers live in that culture, the more familiar and the less peculiar will be the ways of that culture to them. Such is the power of beginnings. The cliché has it that "first impressions are lasting impressions." Introductions and initiations are unique times. They have the potential to shape a subsequent pattern.

This chapter is about beginning pastoral relationships. The topic has been singled out for special attention because it is so influential in shaping subsequent developments. The Christian religion leads us to believe that all human relationships are in the process of becoming; they are not permanently rigid. Yet, like anthropologists in strange circumstances, there are discernible elements in an initiation of a relationship that are present throughout the relationship. In this chapter I will explore the processes of introduction and initiation surrounding a pastoral relationship, with a focused eye on the desirable elements of that relationship purposely present from the outset.

Those processes, including the identification of desirable qualities, are relatively easy to describe to lay people. Every church in the world has done that, does do it, and will continue to do it. The challenge is that various denominational traditions follow differing procedures. Because the intended ends are identical, one can write of those intentions in general terms, applicable to all denominational polities. Individuals may need to make some translations of terms and some revisions of procedure appropriate to their denominational customs.

The communication is greater when the writing embraces a normative pattern and tries to comment on the deviations from the norm that denominational customs produce. For this chapter, the norm will be congregational polity. Polity is a system of church governance. Congregational polity is a local congregation managing its governance without reference to the superstructure of a denomination. (No mainline Protestant church practices pure congregational polity; they all have denominational variations.) The reason for selecting congregational polity is its narrow focus; what is explored here is the way one pastor and one congregation come to have a pastor/parish relationship.

> *Vacant pulpits produce both anxiety and anticipation in the laity.*

There is a pastoral vacancy in your congregation. The laity have come to the necessity of meeting a new pastor in their church. In this circumstance, there are some things that are known, some that are unknown, and some yet to become known. The unfolding of those elements is what introductions and initiations are about.

Begin to understand this unique moment by considering what is already known by the laity. First, the lay people know the recently departed pastor. *What* they know about the previous pastor is quite varied. It is likely that the present attitudes of the laity about their pastoral vacancy range from near despair to near elation. Undoubtedly, some members found the departed pastor a fine minister, one they loved, respected, and valued. These members are worried, to the point of certainty, that the new minister will not measure up to the high standards of the one they have known. Simultaneously, other church members were, frankly, relieved when the pastor left. They had never had an endearing relationship with that pastor, for whatever reason. The church, as they see it, had declined during that pastor's tenure. To use some clichés, these people hope that "new blood" will "turn things around" and that "the new broom will sweep clean."

So, it is known that attitudes toward the clergy already exist, diverse attitudes at that. The deeper significance about this, which is known, is that lay people have attitudes, images, models, ideas, and previous experiences about clergy in general. The role is there, even when the person fulfilling the role is not.

Also known in this transitional moment is that the transitional moment is just that—a transition—and that it will come to a conclusion. Here the time frame varies. Some denominations provide a pastor in the pulpit on the next Sunday; other denominations have a protracted interim—maybe as much as a year—before the successor-pastor arrives. (It is possible that the church is destined to close soon, but if so, there have been warning signs of that.) Most likely the church will survive until another pastor comes. Lay people may adopt a survival mentality in the interim, just hanging on until the new pastor comes. Indeed, that may be the highest goal of the congregation at this transitional moment. One may be surprised at how they do hang together; there is nothing like a crisis to bring out the extra efforts of people. But it is known that, sooner or later, the transition will end and another pastor will come to this church.

The third known quantity is the church itself. The most common, and in some ways the most important, knowledge is that this is a church of Jesus Christ. The laity of this church without a minister may or may not be sophisticated in theology. Whether they speak the language of theology fluently or not, lay people have a sense that this institution is God's institution, that this fellowship aspires to be in fellowship with Christ through fellowship with one another, and that personally and collectively they have a mission to perform. This is reassuring knowledge, for it means that there is some existent consensus about the nature of this institution.

But more, the laity of this church without a pastor know this church. They know it better than the new minister will. They will have to teach the new minister some of what they know about this church. They know that this church has some financial problems; they know that this church has the possibility of a strong youth group in the next several years; they know . . . whatever.

Fourth, they know that their congregation is about to receive some help in their special situation. Long before they were in need of a pastor, a process was working on their behalf. Another church "out there somewhere" had encouraged a person to consider the ministry. A seminary "out there somewhere" with a faculty of Christian teachers had taught students about the ways of God, humanity, and the church. A denominational structure was in place to be of help; denominational people and systems were already functioning on behalf of this congregation.

Finally, it is known that this church is important to these lay people, important to them in diverse ways and for multiple reasons. Because the church is important, these lay people know that this transitional moment is an important moment. Knowing that, they will want to do their best.

On the other side of this transitional moment are some unknowns among the laity. These unknowns center on the new pastor and the future of the church. What will the new minister be like? Will he or she be friendly, kind, fun, helpful? What about our church? Will the new minister call like the former minister did? Will the new minister "keep up" the parsonage? Will the new minister put a stop to the kind of choir anthems we have been having? Lurking beneath these unknowns are some questions that cannot be expressed but are felt nonetheless: Will the new minister bring us God, heal us, save us? In the transitional moment of the church without a pastor these are unknown, but in time they will become known.

While the laity of the church without a pastor ponder these things in their transitional moment, simultaneously "out there somewhere" a different set of questions is forming in the mind of a pastor. This pastor is taking an internal inventory of many things. What has God called me to be and to do? Have I been faithful in that? What do I do best? And there is the question that will trigger action: What will God call me to next?

This pastor has more than personal inventories and personal mission questions in mind. The work to be done, the circumstances for that work, its compensations, and its usefulness are also present. Pastors have chosen, and been chosen for, a career in the leadership of religious institutions. This poses for them some issues not immediately incumbent on the laity; they are questions of religion *and* work. That is the unique combination in pastors: They are religious workers doing the work of religious leadership. When they consider a new pastorate, they will consider it in a combination of religion and work.

Establishing a pastoral relation is like establishing a marriage: There are attraction, courtship, fallings-out, pledges of fidelity, and the development of love and trust.

What will happen next is that the church without a pastor and the pastor "out there somewhere" will begin a process. The process will include three steps: identification and selection, negotiation and establishment, and introduction and inauguration. Each of these is delicate and crucial. Be assured that they *will* take place willy-nilly. I want to offer guidelines of how they can take place in an intentional process aimed at a specific goal.

Start at the end. What does this process intend to accomplish? These guidelines identify a specific goal to accomplish: the establishment of trust between a pastor and a congregation. The goal is meritorious above all others because the health of a religious institution depends on mutual trust. Without that trust, virtually every other hope, aspiration, or intention for the church will wither and fade. Trust is not created by saying, "We will trust each other"; trust is created by a process of growing understanding, respect, and shared life. So, in this transitional moment, both laity and pastor should consider the risks and rewards of seeking a new relationship built on mutual trust.

1. *Identification and selection.* The special ways of denominational customs affect the identification and selection of people for pastorates. The necessary first step for the laity is to review the process of their denomination. Visit with the denominational officer responsible for the local church; he or she will review the customs of the denomination. In addition, the local church has established procedures for the selection of a pastor. (There is a measure of reassurance in knowing that the church has

thought of this and been through it before; its structure assumed change and continuity.)

For purposes of description, let it be assumed that the process involves a representative body of lay members in the church commissioned to present a candidate to the congregation for his or her election as pastor. (Even if the denominational procedure is not as specific as that, still a similar process will take place.)

There are also some preliminary items to be noted. Pastors come in assorted ages, colors, and genders. Today's church is trying consciously to present pastors to congregations without reference to age, race, or gender. The denominational officer will want to make that clear to the church and urge affirmation of equal opportunity for all people.

The next step is to gather documentation on the church. Take a snapshot. (Not literally, although a photo album on the church and community shows a lot that strangers want to know.) Figuratively, a snapshot is an arrested moment in time. It captures the realities present. In other words, assemble data on the church as it is. This activity has two purposes: First, it enables the search committee to have a picture of the whole church, not just the parts individual members know best. Second, the data can be presented to the pastors that the committee meets and talks with about the church.

In addition to the snapshot, the identification of things as they are, the committee should develop a "hope chest," a statement of the needs and desires of the congregation for their church. The broader the base for gathering these hopes, the more authentic they will be. Talk about the church and its future to the whole congregation. Listen to what the congregation says. See if the search committee can distill these hopes into some narrower and more specific statements about what the church wants to become.

The search committee will be pleased to know that pastors have been doing the same thing. Pastors, too, have developed their snapshots and hope chests. These are in the form of ministerial records, dossiers, and applications. This documentation on pastors will become available to your committee.

A cautionary word should be offered here. There is a "truth in advertising" element here. No church will say of itself that it will probably close in three years. Similarly, no pastor will report his or her recent firing. The opinion offered here is that both lay and clergy should understand and accept that this is "best foot forward" on both parts. Obviously, trust is not built on deception. Pastors and churches dare not hide the truth from each other, but this time snapshots and hope chests are communication between strangers.

The next step is a meeting of strangers. Often the first meeting is in the church presently served by the pastor. Members of the committee attend a worship service conducted by the pastor. Reading the snapshots and hope chest of this particular pastor has triggered some initial interest in the search committee, so they go to meet this pastor in person. Although this is a common procedure, there are dangers attached to it. The danger to the pastor is the premature breaking of trust relationships in the pastor's present congregation. The search committee should make its presence known to the pastor *in advance.* The conditions of the visit are strictly visitational, with "no commitment" on either side. The value of this visit is that the search committee can see the style and personality of the pastor. Often a number of these visits are made by the search committee to various churches. The visits usually are educational to the search committee, as they do not know a lot about other churches.

Eventually, one of these visits produces a quickened interest. The next step is a visit by the pastor to the community in which the church is located. Borrowing from the world of business, this is what is known as an "interview." The best interviews are informal conversations. The visiting pastor may want to see the church, the parsonage, the attractions of the community. The purpose of the interview is for strangers to become acquaintances.

Here are some typical areas of conversation between the search committee and a prospective pastor:

Life's Story: This is conversation about where the pastor came from and what has happened in his or her life.

Faith Content: These are conversations about basic beliefs and the style and tradition in which they are couched.

Professional Interests: These are conversations about the ministerial work, including past experience and future expectations.

These conversations will be mutual. The pastor will want to converse with the committee about the church. The pastor's questions will also disclose his or her interests. The interview also is without commitment on either part.

Sometimes one interview is sufficient. Usually, it is not because, in retrospect, both parties think of items they need more time to inquire about. So, a second interview may be arranged. Both parties are free to explore informally and without obligation matters in their interests. The search committee should know that these conversations may be dropped by either party. Also, it is possible that the pastor is conversing with other search committees. Ideally, both the church and the pastor are considering candidates one at a time.

Search committees can become discouraged, especially after they have been rejected. It is like a courtship, but like courtship, one does not always marry the first person with whom one falls in love. In the discouragements, the search committee is learning something about itself and the selection process. Also, during these testing interviews the search committee is coming to know its own collective mind. This is important, for they eventually will have to agree on a candidate they collectively think is the right candidate for their church. Incidentally, the pressure will mount from the rest of the congregation for action; resist it, for conducting this process with dispatch is not nearly as important as conducting it with careful deliberation. Remember the abiding issue: Will this pastor trust us and can we trust this pastor?

2. *Negotiation and establishment.* One never quite knows what makes it happen, but eventually it does: a candidate emerges. The best explanation is that the process was designed to make it happen. The terms of the conversation shift now; they become "iffy." If I become your pastor, the following will be expected, says the pastor. If you become our pastor, the following will be expected of you, says the search committee. At this point either party may say those are unreasonable expectations and cannot be met. Either the expectations are revised or, unfortunately, they are rejected, and the process begins anew.

Trust is now involved in the process. The presence of trust is in specific clarity of expectations. It is best to itemize a job description for the pastor. It is best to itemize the terms of call that the congregation will offer the pastor. It is unwise to leave open some specific desires on either part. Once the relationship is consummated, both sides lose their bargaining positions. Either you will or you won't.

> *The search committee does not quit when the pastor begins. Their next responsibility is the creative assimilation of the new pastor into congregational life.*

The search committee is now authorized to exhibit an unchristian characteristic: Brag about what a splendid job it did! Really, this is part of the process too. What this does is raise the level of expectation in the congregation. Do a "sales job" on the church and on the community. Send out press releases, brochures, word-of-mouth comments about a wonderful development in the congregation.

Also, consider some thoughtful, personal things that can be done for the new pastor. Clean the parsonage, put staples on the shelves. Tell the school that new children will be entering. Gather materials to give to the new pastor. Who are doctors/dentists in town? What is the drugstore? How do you get a driver's license? What newspapers do people read here? The pastor may or may not use the list, but it certainly will be welcome.

Get the internal affairs of the church ready. Make sure the treasurer and trustees know what the financial arrangements are. Make sure the church staff knows what you have discussed about their employment. You may want to plan some all-church party or reception to welcome the new pastor. Do what your church does on festival occasions—a tea, a potluck, a dance, whatever.

When the new pastor has been called, there are two things the search committee should *not* do. Do not relax. Do not draw up a list of miracles for the new pastor to perform. The temptations to do both are great. The reason the committee cannot relax is that its task has been recruitment; now its task is assimilation. It has been doing a task on behalf of the congregation; now it must do a task on behalf of the pastor. The task is to create a climate in the congregation in which the minister can feel at home and a climate in which trust relationships can develop. The temptation to expect miracles is great. The church has struggled without a minister; many have said, "Wait until the new minister comes." Everyone will have a list of unsettled aspects in the life of the church. Do understand that every person in the church, at this beginning point, knows more about those unsettled aspects than the pastor. The pastor is the least equipped person in the church at this point to make crucial decisions. During the initial period of negotiation and inauguration let these matters ride. The greater good is the establishment of the relationship, not the resolution of the vexing problems.

3. *Introduction and inauguration.* The new pastor has come. Everyone was in church for the first sermon. The pastoral search committee was proud and pleased. The congregation seemed to have a spirit of renewal. Everyone knew that a new day had come in the life of this congregation.

The laity may think, "Thank God, that is over." But it is too soon for thanksgiving. What has been accomplished is that a new person has come to the parish. What remains is the establishment of a healthy pastor/parish relationship. The first step toward that health has been taken by following the process of selection and negotiation, but the process of building a trust relationship has just begun.

If the church does not have a constitutional provision for a committee to work with the pastor about matters of pastor/parish concern, now is the time to create such a committee. The church needs it, and so does the new pastor.

The new pastor will be the new pastor until people stop calling him or her "the new pastor." This will probably take about a year. So, there is about a year for the unfolding of the introduction and inauguration stage.

Understand this special moment. Everyone has a new start. The new pastor does not know who the "troublemakers" are; maybe those folks will not be troublemakers in the new shape of things. The congregation does not know that the new pastor has accumulated about twenty-five surefire sermons over the years; the pastor has a chance to develop some new sermons before running out of the old ones. Because the pastor is a community resource, many groups in town will want to meet and hear from this new pastor. Will he or she join the service club? Will the new pastor's family come to the annual Harvest Days festival? Will the new pastor be interested in the United Fund drive?

Almost anything that is new is wonderful, but there will be some snags. Someone forgot to tell the new pastor that under pressure from the fire department the church council pledged five years ago not to have candlelight Christmas Eve services. The new pastor always had a candlelight Christmas Eve service in previous churches. Someone forgot to tell the congregation that the pastor would be in the church office five days a week, not every day. In a new relationship little things arise; this is why a pastor/parish committee is needed right away to keep the molehills from growing into mountains.

It is almost certain that there will be one moment when both the pastor and the congregation fear that they have made a mistake in establishing this pastoral relationship. For the pastor, it may appear in the form of homesickness. He or she will realize that some of the things required here were not required in the previous pastorate and maybe it was better in the old one. Or, more likely, the pastor's family will be engulfed in a surge of homesickness. They may all wish they were back in more familiar surroundings. The pastor may wish he or she had not uprooted everything and everybody to come to this place. This is a normal and natural stirring. Or, the congregation may think it has made a mistake in calling this new pastor. The new pastor refuses to do a children's sermon in the Sunday morning worship. This congregation has always had a children's sermon; the adults love it! The matter went to the pastor/parish committee and still the pastor refused. What kind of pastor do we have here? Were we fooled?

Did we make a mistake? It is a normal and natural stirring. These are the signs of change. In new pastorates there is a large measure of continuity, but there is also discontinuity.

Besides accepting these snags as a natural part of the adjustment process, there is another, more positive, antidote. This first year of introduction and inauguration should have a positive and constructive purpose. In short, the purpose is to do everything possible to become acquainted as a pastor and a congregation. Take the whole year to offer special programs, parties, celebrative worship services. To suggest just a few of these special events, consider an art show, a festival of choirs, a party for every age of the church school, a reception for those who have been members of the congregation for twenty-five years or longer.

In the swirl of these festive events there is also some important information to communicate. The new pastor should have a series of forums in which he or she can speak with every member of the congregation. The pastor should be encouraged to make a presentation on the ministry as he or she intends to practice it in this church. Let the pastor communicate directly about his or her priorities in ministry, tell of how to make use of his or her special skills, tell them what a pastor does all day. Here is the pay-off: The lay members will be pleased to meet their pastor in this way and they will be amazed at all that a pastor does. The information communicated in these forums will not be wasted or forgotten. The process might be reversed, if the pastor is so inclined, so let the lay people invite the pastor to visit them at their places of employment so that the pastor might understand what they do all day.

The visible intention in the inauguration of a new pastorate is responding to change:

The not-so-visible—but very real—intention is to establish trust relationships.

These special inaugural events will take much time and effort. Time and effort in these directions will bring more satisfaction and enduring consequences than the usual initiations. The usual initiation is, while everyone is on good behavior, to attack all the vexing problems plaguing the church. After all, what are ministers here for, some will say, if not to solve the problems.

Understand something about church problems. They have become problems only because they could not be resolved when they first appeared. (If they had been solved, they would not be heard from again.) So, suppose the church follows the conventional way and makes a second or third effort to solve these problems. Suppose by dint of sheer effort the problems are handled. What has been accomplished? Nothing, really. The situation is back to the status quo before the problem developed. If the church fails to solve these vexing problems, it will appear that the new pastor is as ineffective as the former pastors.

Thus, the strategy of the introduction and inauguration is to suspend "business as usual" in favor of an intentional year aimed at becoming acquainted with the new pastor. On the pastor's part, making oneself available, teaching people about who the minister is, what he or she does, meeting them on their "turf" goes a long, long way in establishing trust. On the laity's part, the extension of a genuine welcome, a receptivity to the presence of the new pastor goes a long, long way in establishing trust relationships.

The anthropological researchers' methods are right: What you discover in the initial stages has enduring value.

CHAPTER 6

Ministers Are People

An Exploration of Ministerial Families, Friendships, and "How to Talk to a Pastor"

THE NEXT THREE CHAPTERS deal with the human, personal side of ministers—a helpful balance to the themes of this book. Previously, the central theme has been understanding the unique ministerial role. It is necessary and proper to see ministers in their professional roles. It is also necessary and proper to see the minister as a person, especially in his or her person-to-person relationships. Chapter 2 explores the ministerial personality, but it does so on individualistic terms, asking what are the personality characteristics of people who are pastors. Chapters 6 to 8 explore interpersonal relationships peculiar to the ministerial profession.

These are not uncommon relationships. One way or another everyone has a family, has friendships, engages in small talk. Somehow when those common associations and pursuits are in the context of the ministerial profession they change or are changed by the profession. The quest for understanding in these matters is the quest for how the ministerial image held by lay people permeates, or even distorts, the way lay people understand clergy.

Life in a goldfish bowl is all right for fish; water is their natural habitat. The natural habitat for clergy is the same world in which lay people live.

Like other elements of ministry, there are extremes of life-styles. Normal ministerial life is within the extremes. One extreme is the thoroughly secular life. This extreme would be a life-style indistinguishable from that of an automobile mechanic or an accountant. This extreme embraces the same values, pursues the same ends, and lives by the same rules as every other human creature on God's earth. If they want to pepper their speech with four-letter words, they do. If they want to get roaring drunk on Saturday night, they do. If they desire a summer home on the shore, a boat in the water, a plane in the sky, they pursue these desires too. This extreme identifies with what is accepted, permitted, and valued in society.

The other extreme is virtually anticulture. To give a good word a bad connotation, these clergy are extremely pious. They may never utter an obscenity—even if they whack their thumb with a hammer—they abstain from any form of alcoholic beverage, and they never covet any trinket this affluent society dangles alluringly before them. Their only apparent interest is the trappings of monastic life. Every passion is tamed, every temptation resisted, and any excess well controlled. This extreme rejects and shuns much of what is accepted, permitted, and valued in society.

Neither of these extremes exist in full-blown reality. No person, not even a clergy, is that consistent. Every person shapes his or her life by a plethora of choices over an infinite variety of circumstances. Lay people do that and so do clergy. But here is the difference: *Clergy are both public people and private people.*

Yes, everyone lives in two worlds. Yes, everyone wants

to put his or her best foot forward to the public world and prefers tripping or stumbling in private. But for clergy, the division is not so neat, not so clear, and certainly not so inconspicuous.

For better or worse, lay people expect more of clergy than they expect of themselves. Stated positively, lay people expect clergy to be role models of the Christian life. They want to see incarnate in clergy's public and private lives exemplary models of the Christian life. Stated negatively, lay people expect clergy to be paragons of virtue, never faltering in their virtuosity in public or in private. A novel such as *Elmer Gantry* is typical of a genre of literature that exposes the fallen clergy. Such fiction appeals because of special expectations laid on clergy. The wrongdoing of a clergy person is juicier than the wrongdoing of an automobile mechanic or an accountant because one expects better of a clergy.

There is such a thing as ministerial integrity. Clergy are neither deceitful nor duplicitous. Their commitment to the Christian life is not just vocational. They live their faith in public and in private. They live it by their understandings of what faith requires in public and private expression. Yes, sometimes the pastor's public and private life is at variance with others' expectations. Some of these expectations come and go. Some readers may remember when this society had blue laws regulating life on Sunday. Clergy, and laity too, thought it right and proper not to work on Sunday or go to movies, play games, or dress casually. Those models of decorum have faded.

The issue explored here is expectations about life-styles. The Bible warned against "idols with feet of clay." Any human idol is disappointing. Lay people err when they conjure up a double standard of expectation regarding clergy. Clergy err in not accepting the fact that the double standard exists.

The clergy family: First, it is a family; second, it is people in a family; third, it is people in a family in which there is a clergy person.

Is family life private or public? It is both, but in comparison with the laity, clergy families are more public.

The Protestant tradition accepts a married clergy as opposed to the celibate priests of other traditions. If marriage is a means of grace, argued the Reformers, then clergy should not be denied that means of grace. So Protestants have accepted as normative a married clergy and all that entails: sexuality, financial provision for more than one person, parenting, and the interaction of a family unit with the culture.

The changing role of women has had enormous impact on the clergy family. Not too long ago the phrase "minister's wife" was a title, a role, a status. In its worst manifestation the minister's wife was a source of cheap labor for churches. In many a parish of yesteryear the wife of the pastor was expected to teach Sunday school, sing in or direct the choir or play the organ, serve the women's organization, and generally assist her husband in the care of souls. Now even the phrase is suspect. When a woman is the pastor, the person to whom she is married is not a minister's wife. The unisex word spouse has become popular. A spouse is a husband or a wife, depending on the gender of the pastor.

But more, the old term of minister's wife has lost some of the clarity of the title, the role, and the status. And, yes, in some ways the church has lost a source of cheap labor. The expectations of presence and performance associated with the minister's wife of yesterday have dissipated. Today, more often than not, the minister's wife is employed outside the home. This changing pattern could be due to low pay scales for clergy or it could be due to new opportunities for women; most likely it is both. Lay people do well to consider the special tensions of today's ministerial spouse: He or she has great tension in his or her conflicting roles. He or she is a mate, a worker, a significant person in the institutional church. Undoubtedly, there are peak demands when all three roles simultaneously claim their share of the resources of a solitary person.

By and large, the church and the clergy spouse are the better for the loosening of the rigidities previously imposed on those who were married to clergy. The contemporary flexibility allows clergy spouses, like other lay people, to offer their gifts in the service of the church when appropriate, not when required. The understanding and acceptance by lay people of this change goes far in improving the family life of pastors.

Maturing children seek their own identity. There may be a complicated struggle for that identity when church life imposes rigid identification.

The consequences of married clergy are clergy progeny. Like the minister's wife, in yesteryear, children of clergy had titles, roles, and status. They were known as "PKs," or "Preachers' Kids." In former times, high expectations were also placed on these children. They were role models for subadolescent and adolescent behavior. The special pressure on these children was when their parents coerced them to be role models for other children and not to be just who they were. This coercion virtually guaranteed a rebellion in adolescence. Today the role model coercion is more subtle than substantial. On the positive, healthy side, children of clergy grow up with a greater sensitivity to the life of service, its public and private demands. They usually see themselves as special people in the larger context of church and community. Provided it is not stifling to individuality, their special role is positive and congenial to youthful maturation.

The stresses on the contemporary clergy family are more cultural than ecclesiastical.

Many personal behavioral phenomena previously associated with "the faithless" have come home to the parsonage family. Divorce, alcoholism, drug addiction, illicit sexual relations have penetrated the sanctity of the parsonage, proving that there is no sanctuary from the pressures of social change. The pain of disordered lives is no less painful in ministerial families than in any other family. The pain may be even greater if clergy add a measure of shame to their own—or loved ones'—behavior. Sometimes people in helping professions are isolated in coping with situations in their own lives that need help. The strong sense of "we should be able to work this out ourselves," or the sense of "we should be able to handle this if we have more faith" are sometimes deterrents to allowing help to come from other sources.

Clergy hurt too. Understanding this simple assertion is the most one can expect from lay people about the stresses in clergy families. The parsonage is no ivory tower, no fortress against the slings and arrows of outrageous fortunes. When the slings and arrows of contemporary stress strike the clergy, they hurt, wail, and bleed as others do. The much valued and revered pastoral heart that understands the vicissitudes of life may be the heart that has been wounded itself. If clergy themselves and their families really were paragons of virtue, they would never understand or relate to the rest of us human beings.

Here's a curious dilemma to ponder: Clergy should be friendly but friendless.

The tensions of private and public roles come to bear on a simple element of life: friendship. Lay people think nothing of having "best friends." Best friends are people one enjoys being with. One goes out to dinner with them on weekends; takes a trip with best friends; makes oneself at home in their home. It is a normal, natural part of life—maybe even the most satisfying part. With friends, one is assured that one is not alone; one is part of a human community.

But consider: A minister with best friends is a minister with "favorites," with "cronies," with "that crowd." Clergy are sensitive and vulnerable about personal friendships. Groups within churches have profiles; sometimes the sharpest profile is that of age. If an older pastor relates to his or her peer group, the other, younger groups feel neglected. (Or the older groups feel neglected.) The complaint is usually that of unfair, preferential treatment of one age-group over another.

A pastor to all the people is just that, a pastor to *all* the people. The preferred pastoral decorum for friendships would seem to be "open to all and entangling alliances with none." This decorum shackles the very nature of friendship; it is an entangling alliance. Pastors who become entangled with specific groups in their pastorates may become alienated from other groups.

Clergy pay a price for the tensions of their public and private selves in the matter of friendship. The price is loneliness. To illustrate, one of the values of best friends is that when they get together they can complain about their bosses or the injustices of the office or shop. Such complaining is normal, even therapeutic. Sometimes men friends talk to one another about their wives. Try that out on clergy friendships. Suppose a pastor has a parishioner best friend. Can the pastor complain to that friend about the boss, the unfairness of work, or the spouse? Not likely. The reasons it is not likely are that, first, the friend is part of the church, which is the clergy's boss and perpetrator of working injustices. Second, invariably the friend cannot separate the role from the person. The friend will be stunned that a pastor can have such problems, such thoughts. If friendship is blowing off steam to one who cares, pastors soon learn that parishioners are not their best friends.

Do clergy need a chaplain too?

The delicacies of clergy friendship and the resulting loneliness is resolved in two ways, two ways not always satisfying. When intimate friendships are difficult or denied, clergy will turn to one of two sources for friendship. The most likely one is their spouse. For many clergy, their best friend is their marriage partner. Why not? This person cares about them and understands them and their situation. Like a friend, they will hold their hands, soothe their wounds. Truly no one else in the pastorate knows the pastor's struggles like the pastor's spouse.

The second source of ministerial friendship is other ministers. Like the spouse, a pastoral peer is a ready source of friendship. Other clergy understand the language, the situation, and the meaning of what a fellow or sister pastor says. To tell a professional secret, many clergy associations are built on a game of "Can You Top This?" One clergy will tell another what he or she dares not tell his or her parishioners. The peer reciprocates.

Because of the risks involved in intense friendship with parishioners, clergy tend to have intense relationships with their spouses and their peers.

Friendship with a spouse or peer gives the clergy what true friendship offers everyone: Forgiveness without judgment. All people, even clergy, need to have associations that accept them as they are, not as they appear to be or even hope to be. When they are discouraged and angry, a friend can hear their lament and complaint and, although powerless to change the circumstances, can help them by just hearing the pain, accepting it, and still keeping the relationship intact. Here is the irony: Clergy can do that for parishioners, but parishioners cannot do that for clergy.

The importance of friendship need not be cast in negative terms. It is well and good to have somebody to let off steam to and receive forgiveness and understanding from, but there is also a positive, constructive side to friendship. Charles Schulz, the creator of *Peanuts,* put it this way: "A friend is anyone who likes you . . . and what you like." Friends are leisure-time companions. Golfing partners, fishing companions, concertgoers are friends who share common interest leisure pursuits. Like everyone else, clergy need "good-time buddies" too. But again, people who are that for clergy are more likely to be spouses and peers rather than parishioners.

Lay people should be sensitive to the special dangers of these substitutes for friendship. Being both a spouse *and* a best friend is difficult. The spouse may not always be ready to hear and to forgive. Furthermore, if the cliché that "to have a friend you must be a friend" is correct, clergy are not always that good a friend *to* their spouses. A day filled with people involvement does not bring an evening of happy chitchat with the spouse at home. Husband-wife relationships cannot always take the added burden of best friends too. A pastor can overload the marital relationship by expecting marital satisfactions and best-friend congeniality from the same person.

In a slightly different way the same is true of professional peers. Just because the profession is the ministry is no reason to assume the practitioners are free of competition, jealousy, and outright rejection of one another. In truth, some pastors simply do not like other pastors; this is a human, not a Christian or professional, phenomenon.

The point being made here is a comment about professional loneliness. The usual forms of companionship are complicated for clergy. Their loneliness is often assuaged by intense relationship at home and with peers. But truly isolated is the pastor without response to the needs for human companionship from home or colleague. This pastor will be tempted to make the congregation his or her friend and, in so doing, may diminish the ability to provide the one thing the church needs: pastoral leadership.

Clergy are bilingual: They speak the language of religion and the language of the world.

The last exploration of person-to-person elements in the life of clergy may seem trivial and unnecessary to the laity. It is about how to talk to a pastor. Most lay people never give this a thought; they just open their mouths and speak to their pastors.

This exploration limits the context of conversation with the pastor to casual conversation. When laity speak to pastors about church business or about personal problems, they know how to speak. It may be that most conversations with clergy are about church business or personal problems *because,* in conversations with clergy, lay people are more comfortable with clergy professional language, not personal language.

First, what form of address should lay people use in identifying their pastor? First name? Title? Should children always refer to the church's pastor as "Reverend"?

Here's a revelation to lay people: The pastor knows how the laity see him or her by the names the laity choose to use for him or her. There is a ratio of distance between pastor and parishioner going outward from first name to formal titles. Also, if lay people are about the same age or older, they use first names. If they are younger, they use titles. Children almost always use the title and the last name in referring to their minister. And finally, the more "in" the lay people are in the life of the congregation, the more likely they are to use first names without titles.

There is no precise guideline for how to address a clergy person. In casual conversation, just know that what one calls the pastor communicates who one is and how one sees the pastoral relationship.

Greater than the question of address is the question of content: *What* do you say to a minister? Believe it or not, there are some unwritten rules about casual conversation with clergy. You should never swear within the hearing of ministers and you should not tell bawdy jokes around them. If clergy did not make those rules, why are they around? Why are they widely accepted by lay people? It is an interesting question to explore, given the themes of this book about understanding clergy.

Those prohibitions about casual conversation with the clergy exist because of assumptions about who clergy are and disclose deeply held images of the ministerial personality. Is it not so that one does not swear in the presence of the clergy because such language reveals disrespect for the Deity, and everyone knows clergy are very close to the Deity. Everyone knows that the clergy live in a privatized, isolated world that never hears such expletives.

None of the above is, in fact, true. It is all myth. It is cited here to expose the pervasive power of myths about who clergy are, where they come from, and how they live. The merit, or demerit, of unrefined, coarse speech is one thing; the prohibition against its use because of ministerial myth is something else. The guideline here does not advise one to swear around the minister so he or she knows that they are seen as a "regular guy"; the guideline here is to help lay people understand that they hold myths about clergy. The proof of this is the converse: Let a clergy person swear like a drunken sailor and check out the negative lay reaction! Such language does not fit the myth.

By far the most serious issue in casual conversation with

clergy is lay assumptions about what interests clergy. The pastor's public religious role is so clearly defined that lay people assume that what interests ministers is religion and only religion.

In this regard there is one insult that some lay people inflict on clergy. When some lay people want to explain something to a pastor, they search for religious metaphors to explain it. "Why, Pastor," they say, "it's like preaching on Easter Sunday." It is not. No matter the point, the metaphor is invariably wrong and discloses shallow religious understanding on the part of the speaker. Yes, clergy do understand religious metaphors. (This is a good reason not to use them.) But more important, clergy can understand other things without reference to religious metaphor. They are neither dumb nor single-minded.

Some lay people clip articles out of newspapers. They bring any newspaper article that has to do with religion to their pastor. They never bring a food or fashion item. Why? Everyone knows it is religion and religion alone that interests clergy. (Incidentally, experienced clergy know that just about any newspaper story on religion is either wrong, slanted, or irrelevant.) Again, the act of communicating or sharing communication is not involved here. What is involved is the assumptions about what interests clergy. Do not narrow and compartmentalize their interests.

Swiss psychiatrist Paul Tournier wrote a wonderful book entitled *The Meaning of Gifts.* In the book he explores the depths and heights of symbolic interpersonal meanings represented by the simple act of giving a gift. Each gift discloses a whole series of assumptions about who the giver is, who the other is, and the nature of the relationship that exists between the two. In a literal sense, lay people give gifts to clergy. Inevitably, the lay people give clergy gifts with religious dimensions. (Most clergy have shelves of Bibles that lay people have given them on one occasion or another.) The literal gifts of a religious nature reveal the laity's mythic assumptions of who clergy are.

Conversation is a gift too, a nonmaterial gift of time, care, and interpersonal sharing. The best way to converse with a clergy person is out of your authentic self. What interests you? What wisdom do you have in you? What are you afraid of? What do you hope for? The authentic self of the minister will hear and understand because of his or her own personal authenticity. Do not use the language of religion or the metaphors of religion to communicate with a religious person. This compartmentalizes and specializes both the content of the communication and the person to whom it is communicated. Religion and religious people are not so easily categorized. Speak of life, all of it, and you will speak of religion.

CHAPTER 7

Normal Changes in Pastor/Parish Relationships

An Exploration of Births, Achievements, Anniversaries, Resignations, and Retirement During Pastor/Parish Relationships

THIS CHAPTER, LIKE THE PRECEDING ONE, explores the human elements in pastoral ministry, the personal aspects of parish life. Whereas chapter 6 solicited the understanding of the laity about unique dimensions of interpersonal relationships accompanying pastoral work, this chapter explores a variety of circumstances that *may* occur during a pastoral relationship.

The set of circumstances explored in this chapter may be understood by the same theory as in chapter 6: Pastors, like lay people, have a private side of life and a public side. But the role and image of the pastor makes private events more public. Also, because a pastor is a visible and significant person to the whole congregation, the issue of how religious institutions respond to pastoral circumstances is, of necessity, explored in this chapter. (How pastors handle these circumstances is another matter.)

One disclaimer seems appropriate to cite at the outset.

Congregational responses to circumstances of change in pastors' lives vary with the nature of the congregation. Some congregations—usually, but not always, those that are smaller and more rural—have an intense and intimate congregational life. If trauma enters the life of one member, it enters the lives of many members. Other congregations—usually, but not necessarily, those that are larger and more urban—are less intense, more scattered in their fellowship. A trauma to one is not always known and borne by all. The degree of communal response also varies with situations, affected by individual personalities and length of tenure. In short, although these guidelines are presented as if there were one appropriate response by a congregation to changes in their pastor's life, there are, in fact, many forms of response appropriate to particular congregations.

Despite the varieties of congregational responses, there is an overarching necessity for attempting to explore these guidelines. Pastor/parish relationships are never static; they are always dynamic. Just when a congregation thinks it has reached a level of trust and understanding with its pastor, *zoom, boom,* a new element disturbs the equations of trust and understanding. Depending on the magnitude of these changes, the parish may find itself in another dimension of pastor/parish relationships.

In this chapter, too, it is helpful to recall the earlier depiction of vertical or career patterns, and horizontal or terms of pastoral covenants with congregations, in ministerial life. For example, the resignation or reassignment of a beloved pastor from one congregation to another pastorate may be interpreted as a betrayal and rejection of the congregation by the pastor. Understanding that pastors also have career patterns impinging on their decisions may take some of the sting out of what seems a personal rejection. Many, but not all, changes in pastoral circumstances are related to the vertical dimensions of career alterations, but inevitably, they have impact on the horizontal, parish relationships.

> *A normal change in a pastor's life is a change that any other person might have, but because of the public side of the pastor's life, such changes precipitate congregational response.*

Further, there are two kinds of change: normal and unwelcome. The two may be one, as in the death of a pastor while serving a congregation. But for purposes of discussion, it is important to differentiate between normal and unwelcome changes. I will begin with a series of changes that come under the category of normal changes and consider guidelines for congregational response to these normal changes.

A child is born to the parsonage couple. Many people become parents; this is not unique. But the parents' public roles make that parsonage birth unique. In a way the whole congregation become godparents to the newborn. Good, let it happen! The affirmative response of the congregation communicates to the clergy-parents a sense of acceptance and support by the congregation. It would not be unusual for the pastor to request that some other pastor perform the ritual of baptism for the newborn. Why? Because the pastor is clarifying his or her own role: He or she wants to be a parent, not a pastor, to the child.

Congregations served by pastors who become parents for the first time should brace themselves in two ways. Brace first for a barrage of sermon illustrations about children. The wit and wisdom of the minister's child will continue unabashed until the child becomes old enough to see that what he or she considers private is being made public by his or her parent. Take heart, the illustrations will stop when that happens. Brace, too, for a new dimension in the pastor/parish relationship. First, the congregation will have a rival for the pastor's time and interest; second, the parsonage may seem too small, the salary, inadequate; and third, the pastor will become more future oriented, thinking more of his or her career. After all, parents have more to think about than each other and their work. This is predictably natural, but natural or not, the terms of pastor/parish relationships change when young pastors become parents for the first time. Fear not. As long as there have been married clergy, churches and pastors have adapted to the demands of clergy's playing more than one role in life.

A pastor with an advanced degree is like a flashy car with no motor: It looks good, but where will it take you?

Many pastors inaugurate and complete a program of advanced study during a pastorate. That, too, produces change, normal change. The congregation may have committed itself to having a pastor who for several years undertakes scholarly pursuits in addition to parish work. This necessitates a shift in time, energy, and resources by the church and the pastor. But when the advanced study is complete, who shares the joy of accomplishment, who offers the rewards of advancement?

The first question is easier to answer than the second. It would not be unreasonable to negotiate an expectation with a pastor pursuing an advanced degree along these lines: Stay in this pastorate as long after you receive the degree as you took to achieve it. By all means, the congregation should join with the pastor in celebrating the accomplishments of advanced study. Have a great party! It will not happen every year, so have an exceptional celebration.

But keep this in mind: Whether or not it is demonstrably true, a pastor who completes advanced study considers himself or herself more qualified than before undertaking the study. Teachers in public schools have salary increments built into the grid of compensation. Clergy do not have a policy in this regard, but be assured that pastors, like teachers, will expect recognition of their advanced degrees. Whatever those expectations are, if they are not forthcoming from the present pastorate, the itch to have a pastorate that recognizes these advancements will be scratched.

Pastors have significant anniversaries that ought to be recognized and celebrated. Take, for example, the twenty-fifth anniversary of an ordination. What chance for celebration and change does this milestone portend? Most assuredly, it will start some introspection on the pastor's part. What have I accomplished with my life? Am I doing the same thing now that I did before, at about the same level as when I began? These introspections will surface in the pastoral mind because of the absence of a professional measuring device. Pastors do not know how to evaluate their own success or lack thereof. Such is a good time for lay people to join the pastor in an examination of their roles and agreements in the local church. Maybe as simple a gesture as extra weeks of vacation will symbolize a quarter of a century of service to the whole church. The reason these milestones are hard for lay people to grasp creatively is the excess of the horizontal dimension. They will say, "But this pastor has been in our congregation for only two years. Why should we recognize twenty-five years of service by changing our terms with the pastor?"

As sensitive and caring as lay people can be about their pastor's well-being, they invariably miss the significances of career milestones for pastors. Even in the most cooperative denominational structures, one congregation does not perceive how other congregations share in pastoral careers. This is unfortunate, for it plays havoc with ministerial careers. Until the day comes when all wrongs are set right, the best guideline for the laity of a particular congregation is to remind them that the pastor they presently relate to has a history of previous parish relationships. They are stewards of that history too.

More staff solves some old problems but brings some new ones.

Changing staff is another instance of change in a pastor's relationship to a parish. This circumstance applies most directly to large, multiple-staff congregations. But it also has implications for churches with part-time custodians, secretaries, and choir directors. The addition of new staff is fraught with disillusionment for everyone. Coping with this change requires great sensitivity.

Suppose the ministerial tasks have become more than one person can handle. The pastor needs help. Inevitably, everyone looks forward to the great day when there will be more help in the leadership of the church. The whole vision of this change is a salutary one: more help to reduce everyone's burden.

So dominant is this vision that it never occurs to anyone that *everyone's* role and pattern of relationships change when the help arrives! Someone must become the supervisor of the new worker. When churches expect the pastor to oversee the church staff, as they usually do, this means that the pastor has an important job change: He or she is now a supervisor of others—in addition to his or her own work. Further, no matter how small or large the church, a team of paid staff is just that: a team. When one member of the team is replaced, every other member of the team is affected. The result? A new shake, a new pattern of relationships for all. A new staff member, no matter how necessary and welcome, is fruitbasket upset for the whole church. Every church with a multiple staff has gone through this change. It can be done. The best guideline to lay people is to anticipate disillusionment. What seems a solution, and in fact often is a solution, also introduces new complications.

When a pastor resigns, a grief process will ensue for the pastor and the congregation.

When a pastor concludes a pastorate, great changes are initiated. The first of these is the initiation of grief work. Just as a funeral for a deceased person facilitates the healing power of "grief work," so the termination of a pastorate must facilitate that grief work. Call the resignation "closure" to understand the dynamic of this change. The purpose of closure is to signal a new reality for everyone. The pastoral relationship is dead and must be buried. Forget about resurrection, which is sure to come. Closure is final things that pastors and congregations can do.

The following are forms of closure. First, some straight talk to each other about what has been lacking, what has been accomplished, and what comes next. The straight talk ranges from clearing the air over some unresolved conflicts to factual information about the process for replacement. Second, there must be personal and ceremonial expressions of good-bye. A congregational event honoring the departing pastor should be held. Often a monetary gift, called "a purse," is solicited from the congregation. Pastors and laity should express to each other the gratitude that they have for the past relationship. Third, a renewal of faith should be incarnated in the farewell proceedings. When the trust relationship between a pastor and a congregation is broken, it becomes evident that their trust relationship represented a larger, enduring relationship. Both the pastor and the congregation have a trust relationship with Christ and the universal church. In closure this covenant must be reaffirmed. Yes, a pastor and a congregation may now walk separate ways, but both are on the part of Christ and the church.

The failure to close with finality a pastoral relation promises to both pastor and congregation a snare and a trap in the next set of relationships. If there has not been closure, neither will have let go, and in the next new set of circumstances they will hang on to what has been, deterring them from what is possible in the new relationship.

> *Any pastor who is loved and admired by the whole congregation is a pastor who has been away from that congregation for about five years.*

There is one other normal pastoral change expressed as a resignation. This is the retirement of a pastor. This change, too, calls for special understanding. In this circumstance, congregations confront two phenomena: the loss of a pastor from their congregation and the conclusion of a ministerial career.

The laity's understanding of changes wrought by pastoral retirement may be deepened by a secret personal opinion: Pastors are scared to death of retirement. It is human nature to be scared of it. If they are not scared, they are, at least, ambivalent. As pastors contemplate their retirement, one part of them is eager for the cessation of certain functions they will easily—and in some cases gladly—renounce. Another part of them approaches retirement not so easily or gladly.

Understand their feelings of dread or ambivalence. In chapter 1 a distinction of clergy work was made between ministerial presence and performance. Retirement means the end of both; pastors know that. They can handle the cessation of functions. Either they are weary of them or they know they will have some limited opportunities to function as pastors even in retirement, as interim ministers, guest preachers, professionals invited for certain occasions. But the loss of ministerial presence, the myths and mystiques congregations project on their pastors, this is something else.

Through forty years of service the ministerial presence has become part of their being. It is inevitable that it would become their identity, their reason for being, the purpose of existence. It is terrifying to contemplate life without it. The terror is unrealistic, but it really is there.

The dread of the loss of ministerial presence grows out of some unique aspects of pastoral work developed previously in this book. The life and work of clergy is *communal.* They work with groups. Retirement is the loss of communal status. Pastors tend to be dependent personalities. In forty years they have become dependent on those horizontal dimensions. They are secure in their personhood by the horizontal associations of a pastorate. Specifics of that dependency abound: the parsonage—they must move from the parsonage now; the anomaly of working on Sunday—many retired clergy must become accustomed to attending worship with their spouses, something they have not done in forty years; the managerial role—who now will seek their counsel, their wisdom?

There are other positive, healthful aspects to ministerial retirement, but they belong in another book. In this book, aimed at the increased understanding of pastors by lay people, facing retirement is explored. Given the darker sides to ministerial retirement, these guidelines are appropriate.

> *A retiring minister is not quitting work: The minister is relinquishing perceptions of self, authority, and status.*

1. Long before retirement is an issue, clarify policy of church expectations. Some policies are denominational,

some are governmental. Most clergy pension plans are designed to coincide with social security. Under present law this is age sixty-five but changing. The policy should not be designed for the benefit of an individual minister, but for the good of the whole church. The existence of a policy establishes a perimeter. This perimeter lets all know when it is being approached or transgressed.

2. Offer the retiring clergy a double honor—honor not only for the service to a particular church, but also for the career now terminating.

3. Insofar as it is within your power (and understand it is a limited power) do not let your pastor retire to nothing. Pastors must retire to something. Were it at all possible, a caring church would let the last several years of a pastor's active ministry be spent pursuing, in tentative and experimental ways, a hobby, interest, or second career that might become important in retirement.

4. Never allow a pastor who is eligible for retirement benefits to subsidize your congregation by staying in the pastorate, collecting a pension while working at reduced pay. It is tempting to both the pastor and congregation to do so. In yielding to the temptation, the church always loses.

5. In kindness, communicate the realities of retirement to the pastor. There is no guilt or shame attached to retirement. Religiously, the meaning of one's life is not serving Christ's church. There are other forms of serving Christ besides being a pastor of a church. (Lay people *really* know that!) A new world will begin, not end, when the pastor retires.

6. Demonstrate that the admiration in which he or she is held is personal, not just ecclesiastical. Welcome the pastor into the wonderful world of the laity; this is where he or she came from.

7. Keep the retired pastor away from his or her former church. Lay people can help this enormously. Do not re-

quest ministerial services from a retired pastor when your church has a new minister. If you must, always communicate your desires through the new pastor.

Successful retirement of clergy is a compensatory process. The compensation of satisfaction for forty years of service is the laity's to give. Compensation for alternative involvements is the clergy's to find. Compensation for a full life of service is God's grace to humanity. Do not confuse the compensation or whose they are to give.

CHAPTER 8

Unwelcome Changes in Pastor/Parish Relationships

An Exploration of a Pastor's Death/Disability, the Dismissal of a Pastor, and a Divided Pastorate

THE FOREGOING CHAPTERS explored unique elements of clergy life-style and coping with normal changes in the course of pastor/parish relationships. This chapter continues by diving into troubled waters. Unwelcome changes do occur in pastor/parish relationships, and this chapter explores their murky manifestation.

The descriptive words are chosen carefully: "unwelcome change." The changes are unwelcomed by the laity; they are unwelcomed by clergy. They are unwelcome to both because they violate the purposes and intentions of both.

In every pastor/parish relationship there are hassles and haggles, disruptions and disputes, even accusations and acrimony. Conflict is as much a part of life as birth and death. But reconciliation, too, is as much a part of life as birth and death. Churches believe in, preach, and teach reconciliation as a part of Christian life.

Conflict and reconciliation abound in churches—even in

healthy churches, even in trusting pastor/parish relationships. Learning how to cope with conflict, learning how and when to give and receive reconciliation are symptoms of health. Parent/child, husband/wife, and pastor/parish are all relationships lived in the processes of conflict and reconciliation.

How do we know when change is unwelcomed? An unwelcome change in pastor/parish relationships is when the change consumes the participant's time, energy, and emotion to the exclusion of everything else. Welcome changes are assimilated into the continuum of life; unwelcome changes block the normal flow of everything else. If a rupture comes on a pastor and a parish, neither can continue forward until the rupture seals. So there is a magnitude of proportion about unwelcome change; it is never trivial or bothersome. It is catastrophic, calling into question everything else.

> *If disruptions could be fixed, with everything returning to the status quo, it was not change. If someone is not better off as the result of change, it is unwelcome.*

The definition of unwelcome change, then, is a development in a pastor/parish relationship that stifles all other elements of the relationship, demanding attention to this matter of great importance.

The sudden and unexpected death of a beloved pastor is an example of unwelcome change; this meets the criterion. It happens. Death is no respecter of professions. Maybe the death was not sudden and unexpected; there were months or years of warning. And maybe it was not death at all; maybe it was debilitating circumstances. These changes may have come rapidly, as fast as a car on a slippery road runs a stop sign. Maybe the debilitation came slowly, a deteriorating physical condition that was pretty good one day and not so good the next, moving ever downward in a descending spiral of shrinking vitality. This happens too.

A church with a recently deceased or irreparably disabled pastor is a church with unwelcome change. The magnitude of the unwelcome change is great; everything in the life of the church is clouded. The previous advice about healthy churches and trust relationships is put aside by this catastrophe. Or is it?

In the circumstances of a deceased or disabled pastor, the laity have come on a new context in which to seek and express the health and trust of Christian community. Although death and disability of a pastor are different events, they have a common impact on the laity of the church: Expectations must be revised.

Leaving aside the processes of grief that are sure to accompany such an unwelcome change, lay people have additional considerations. The first is common decency. The first and immediate goal for the laity, beyond their own grieving for the person lost to them, is common decency. The Christian church is not a heartless, thoughtless, uncaring institution. It was for times such as these that Christian compassion was conceived.

There are two objects of this common decency: the surviving family and each other. A highly likely condition of the pastor's family—and each other—is the concurrent conditions of anger, pain, and sorrow. Lay people may add sympathy, which is sorrow for another. Know that these are not normal, typical, desired conditions. Also know that they are not eternal. In every human being there is a healing process; everyone adjusts to new realities in his or her life. Knowing that and working constructively for it is the healthy part of this unwelcome pastor/parish relationship.

The acts of common decency may be financial. Have the survivors been provided for through insurance? Most congregations insure pastors so that their survivors will have some measure of financial security in the event of the death or disability of the pastor. If your particular congregation has not been far-sighted enough to do this, common decency requires an immediate search for resources, either from denominational emergency funds or from governmental agencies.

Then, for some congregations, there is the question of occupancy in the parsonage. If lay people had never thought of providing a parsonage as being potentially harmful, these circumstances will make them see the church-owned home in a new light. Common decency requires that nothing be done about the parsonage immediately. But the prospect of years and years of survivors in a parsonage, even after another minister has come, has threatening implications for churches. Evicting widows and orphans is not seemly to churches. On the one hand, selling the parsonage to the survivors could be common decency. On the other hand, giving the parsonage to the survivors may not be common decency to the whole congregation and its future. Making the best of a bad situation should become everyone's goal, and after a decent interval—how long is that?—the congregation must decide on some next steps.

In the death or disability of the pastor more than common decency is at stake. There is certain to be an expression of anger on the congregation's part. Why did this have to happen? A religious community will certainly reexamine its faith. Why did God let this happen to our pastor? (If the question is strictly theological, which it is not, the answer is that God did not just let it happen; God shares the pain of the loss.) The angry questions prompt a guideline: A church having a trauma such as this should have an interim pastor. An interim pastor is helpful in this situation because everyone knows the interim is a caretaker-pastor—what a great adjective for this special ministry: "caretaker"! A sensitive interim pastor will help the congregation to realize that they are not being punished by the wrath of God and that the life of the church goes on.

The final guideline to the congregation is to sit tight with an interim minister for a while. The circumstances have been unfortunate; the misfortune will be compounded by rushing to find a replacement pastor. Why? Because the next pastor will not be a replacement for the fallen pastor. Until the congregation has made progress in its grief work, is accepting a new reality in its life, no pastor will do. Limp along until strength comes back into your legs. It will . . . in time.

If God does not see fit to remove a pastor, should a church?

Turn now to another unwelcome change. This unwelcome change is quite different from the death or disability of a pastor, but the similarity is the removal of a pastor from a pastorate. In the crass argot of the day, this is "firing." In more institutional language, it is "dismissal." Stretching credibility to its breaking point, it is "making a pastor available for a greater opportunity." Any way it is put, the trust level is nonexistent and the pastoral covenant is dissolved.

When these changes present themselves, everyone should know the name of the estate: It is "the last resort." It is pursued *only* when all previous resorts have failed. This means communication has broken, negotiation has failed, and reconciliation has been rejected.

Two procedural checks are recommended before dismissal. First, the denominational officer responsible for this local congregation must be informed. The officer may attempt a last-ditch reconciliation, but if this fails, the officer will explain the denominational procedures for dismissing a pastor. Second, the constitution or pertinent church rules governing the dismissal of a pastor must be consulted. Frankly, both steps make it difficult to dismiss a pastor. They should. The dismissal of a pastor should be with the concurrence of the *congregation,* not just a few members.

It may stretch credibility, too, but the dismissal of a pastor can be an act of healthy pastor/parish relationships. It is healthy when a pastor is engaged in self-destructive behavior that requires professional help and the help has been refused. A church that keeps a pastor under those conditions contributes to the pastor's self-destruction, condoning unacceptable behavior as it were.

Face it: There are irresponsible pastors. They need not be tolerated by the church any more than an embezzler must be kept employed in the bank because the embezzler is qualified for the job and needs the work.

Yes, some pastors should be dismissed. There is a procedure to do so. The congregation need not feel excessively guilty about a development it could not help. As easy as that is to understand, the other side must also be understood. The pastor of a local church is vulnerable. A handful of lay members who, for whatever reasons, want a pastor removed can make it difficult for that pastor. The removal reason may be trivial, such as the minister's looks or manner. It may be consequential, such as the pastor took a stand contrary to the wishes of the handful. This is why a dismissal *must be* difficult for a congregation to accomplish. Were it not difficult, church life would be a tyranny of the minority.

An outright dismissal should be crisp and clean. The church records must show due cause and declare what steps were taken (and rejected) for reconciliation. A terminal date should be set. It is customary to negotiate severance pay. Both time and finance should be sufficient to allow a dismissed minister opportunity to find another position.

Like a church with a deceased or disabled pastor, a church that dismissed a pastor should have an interim pastor after the dismissal. Whatever the circumstances of the dismissal of one pastor were, the succeeding pastor will have great difficulty in establishing a trust relationship.

Lay members should know that the process leading up to the dismissal of a pastor is never neat and clean. It is always very, very messy. The parishioners who have concluded that "the pastor must go" will be amazed to learn that there are other parishioners who think dismissal is uncalled for. "Pro" and "con" encampments may be established. The conflict between these groups will escalate. In such extreme circumstances, combatants lose sight of the issues and unleash personal attacks. It is pathetic to see pro and con camps at prayer, each invoking God's support for its own efforts. This is why long intervals of interim ministry are needed; these personal wounds take a long time to heal.

> *The outright "firing" of a pastor occurs infrequently; more common are the pressures on a pastor to resign.*

Pastors are not dismissed by neat and tidy ways. More common than outright firings are pressures to resign, avoiding blatant firing. Church members have withheld participation, finance, and common decency to force a pastor's resignation. A pastor may choose to resign on seeing that he or she cannot govern. These pressures for resignation have more impact, in the long run, on the church than they have on one particular pastor. From henceforth the church will be scarred by threats of withdrawal if the expectations of the threateners are not met. Inadvertently, the institution has ceased to be a church and has become instead a barroom brawl with big sticks wielding order.

In these last-resort conditions, here is a better guideline: The pressures on the pastor should be those of clearly defined expectations of performance, not threats to withdraw. A church will survive high expectations, not threats.

There is no other way to put it: The only alternative to these unwelcome changes is constant and intentional attention to the trust relationship, the constant flow of communication through a pastor/parish committee, a broad-based understanding of what together lay and clergy are trying to accomplish.

When is the whole less than the sum of its parts?
When the whole is a whole church divided into
unreconciled parts.

The third unwelcome change in pastor/parish relationships is a divided church. Magnitude is again the sign of unwelcome change. All churches have subgroups within the larger group of the whole congregation. This is not the issue here. The existence of subgroups without a common loyalty to Christ and this church is the issue. Divisive groups have individual expectations and agendums; they function as if they were the whole church. Possibly the cause of the divided church is the pastor, but more likely the divisions are rooted in previously unresolved conflicts of principle, purpose, or faith.

Assuming a divided church was not directly precipitated by the pastor, laity should know of the special stresses divided churches place on pastors. In the attempt to exercise his or her mediating personality traits in the cause of reconciliation, the pastor of a divided church struggles to hold the contending groups in fellowship. Assume the divisive issues are theological, the divisions are between so-called liberal or progressive factions and so-called conservative or reactionary groups. These divisions are stressful for the pastor because of the pastor's multiple roles within the congregation. As a theologian, the pastor has a stance of his or her own on theological issues. It is tempting to side with those who are "right." But the pastor's heart seeks unity and concord among the members.

A creative guideline is to approach theological divisions as matters of conscience, helping each side respect the conscience of the other. Admittedly, this is a temporary solution, because these differing consciences will express themselves in the policies and directions of the church.

Some church members, for the good of the church, should leave it.

Taking a worst-case scenario, a congregation that is permanently and hopelessly deadlocked on every aspect of its life, is a church that has come on unwelcome change. What do pastors and laity do when they have come to a perpetually divided state? They admit a fact to each other: By their unresolved differences, they have ceased to be a church. Because their division has not yielded to reconciliation, they can no longer be agents of reconciliation.

These three explorations are cut from the same cloth. Unwelcome change brings a theory: A church breaks when trust is broken. Extremities, last resorts, and worst cases are circumstances in which restoring what has been lost becomes the primary reason for being. Maybe what these dour circumstances underline for every church member is how essential the trust relationship is in churches and how its neglect puts the church in peril.

EPILOGUE

How to Tell Whether or Not a Pastor/Parish Relationship Is Healthy

THE WORD HEALTH has appeared frequently in this book. It is an appropriate word to use; it is even descriptive of pastor/parish relationships.

Health is a corollary to a central biblical image. The church is described as "the body of Christ" in the New Testament. The usual meaning of that metaphor is that differing parts of the human body function independently but, at the same time, contribute to the overall functioning of the whole body. The many references in this book to varieties is consistent with that metaphor. There is no one way to live and work together in the Christian community; there are many communities and many ways of working together. Types of churches abound. So, too, do types of clergy. If one contemplated only the varieties, one would despair of the church ever existing, serving, or thriving.

There is, however, a corollary to the biblical metaphor of the church as a body. The corollary is health/disease. The body of Christ, like the human body, struggles to be healthy. This, too, is frequently asserted in this book. In one sense, health is the absence of disease. Until recently, medical science has studied disease, assuming that the control or eradication of disease would increase bodily health. Now another perspective has emerged. Instead of asking what ails us, the new approach assumes a state of health and examines factors contributing to the state of health as opposed to the factors of disease.

The biological presuppositions are fascinating. Disease is "out there," very real, very dangerous, ever posing menacing threats to well-being. But humanity survives! People navigate their way through a disease-ridden environment. Within the body itself are disease-resisting resources—immunities, antibodies, regenerative processes. An open wound must be treated with antiseptics lest the bacteriologic disease enter the healthy body and take lodging in it. In physiological terms, the human body survives a threatening world through its disease-prevention resources.

This is the operational metaphor of this book. It is an application of medical presupposition to the church, the body of Christ. The possibility of disease in the body of Christ is as varied and as great as it is menacing and virulent. Many things can go wrong in churches. Sadly, many things do go wrong in churches. But if one contemplates only the possibilities of disease, one is amazed and awestruck by the two-thousand-year survival of the church. There must be an ecclesiastical immune system too.

In effect, this book is research into the immune systems of the church. What are the processes that work and are at work for church health in a menacing world? This treatise has advanced a hypothesis: The source of health in churches is trust. As I have asserted, it is a disease resister of churches. One hastens to add that there are other, many other, disease fighters: faith, grace, hope, love, and all those good words of the Christian tradition.

Based on the assumption of trust as a disease-resistant presence in churches, the prescriptions for the establishment of health have been those leading to the increase of trust between pastors and congregations.

The prescription for the preservation of health through trust has been the advancement of understanding. What is not understood is menacing too. But more positively, what is understood is trustworthy. My goal has been to roll back some of the barriers of misunderstanding between laity and clergy. If I have erred, I have erred by overstating the human side of clergy. The possible error, to use a phrase from biblical scholarship, has been to demythologize the role and person of the pastor.

It jolts sensibilities, for instance, to discuss ministerial careers. Does the Bible allow for careers? Isn't the life of servanthood enough? Why clutter the simple good with complications of hierarchical advancement? The reason is that they are there. The cluttering and complication were not invented in this book. Too often, in churches, the name of the game is to pretend that complications do not exist.

Pretending that complications are not there leads to ill health. Pretending that clergy are not human also leads to ill health. The menace in contemporary churches is the pretense that members know who clergy are and what they are trying to do. Striking down that pretense, demythologizing the clergy myth, has been a prescription of this book.

Understanding is a process and not an estate. I have advanced a number of theories about who clergy are and what they do. What if those theories were out-and-out wrong? What if they were not so much wrong as one-sided or partially right and partially wrong? That would be unforgivable—if understanding were an estate and these specifics were the only passages to understanding clergy. The forgiveness of these errors, their correction and replacement is the process of understanding. Understanding does not have to exist in one form, at one level, by one formulation. The process of understanding goes ever onward.

In local churches the processes of understanding are in the hands, mouths, and hearts of pastors and laity. They work together, talk together, love together. This book, with all its theories, prescriptions, guidelines, formulated understandings, is a stimulus to those pastors and lay people. Much as a physician's pill activates one's own resistance, so this book provokes the processes of health already present in congregations.

Pastors and lay people must understand each other. They must understand each other to trust each other. They must trust each other for the church to be healthy. This is the theory. The application of that theory is not its articulation in a book. The application is in the day-to-day life of pastor/parish relationships. This is where, and only where, understandings must be formed. The elemental questions of laity and clergy are, Who are we and what are we trying to accomplish together? Historically, these are questions of church order and mission. The healthy church is the church that understands that these are the pertinent questions and attends to them.

Finally, what are the signs and symbols of healthy churches? How do we know where we are in the process of understanding one another? How can one tell if the trust levels are high.

There are some false and erroneous signs and symbols of the presence of these things. Peace and concord are two of these. Just because friction and division are signs of the absence of trust and confused understanding, it does not follow that peace and concord are signs of the presence of trust and understanding. Prosperity and growth may be false also. Again, the absence of these may portend the absence of trust and understanding, but conversely, the presence of growth and prosperity does not mean the understandings are resolved. More likely it means that both pastor and congregation have agreed to submerge these pursuits, preferring to attend to other, more pressing demands. The submersion is temporary. The processes of trust-building and the quest for understanding can lie dormant for some time, even years, but they will surface, clamoring for air, demanding attention.

No, outward and visible signs do not indicate a healthy church based on mutual trust and understanding. One must look elsewhere for the evidence of trust and understanding.

The signs and symbols of health are in the quality of the relationships within the parish regardless of the external circumstances. Can the laity talk with one another openly and with respect? Can the laity accept differences and disagreements? Can conflict be resolved through negotiation and reconciliation and losers do not feel like outcasts when they have lost?

The two certain signs of quality in pastor/parish relationships are creative coping and celebrative events. Creative coping by churches is coming to grips with the realities of the situation in which churches find themselves. Much waste goes on in churches that wish they were something else other than what they are. Churches have a certain restlessness. Another place, another program, another minister, another . . . whatever, anything but what is, will save us. But creative coping is not wasteful. Instead of lamenting what is not, it accepts what is and copes with it. Creative coping is not the counsel of preserving the status quo. Churches, like people, must change and grow. So, creative coping is more creative than it is coping. Quality pastor/parish relationships are those in which freshness, innovation, experimentation are not dirty words. We trust each other enough to try. We understand each other so well that we will undergo mutual risks together. In quality pastor/parish relationships, the energies and the resources are not only replenished, but also utilized in coping creatively with the particular circumstances.

The second sign and symbol of quality pastor/parish relationships is visible in celebrative events. This is not the counsel of dancing in the ballroom of the sinking *Titanic.* There is a time and a place for everything, even a time to dance and to refrain from dancing. Rather, this counsel is for the affirmation of life, of life together in Christ's church. Quality pastor/parish relationships are life-affirming. Pastor and parish are grateful to God for life itself and especially for life together. The psalmist said, "I was glad when they said to me, 'Let us go to the house of the Lord!' " (Psalm 122:1). Religion is not a category of life. Religion is life. The church is where life is found in all its woes and exhaltations. In this book I have frequently advised parties, celebrations, and "coming together" for festivals. Why? Because festival moments are occasions to express love and concern for one another. Church celebrative events are love and care for one another in the name of, and for the sake of, Christ. Even somber events—a funeral, a farewell to a departing, beloved pastor—are celebrative events; they lift up all of life in praise of God and thank God for mercies and grace through all of life.

The approaches to understanding, the affirmation of trust relationships, the signs and symbols of quality and health have been stated. Let the conversation continue.